How to
Involve Parents
in Early Childhood Education

How to
Involve Parents
in Early Childhood Education

Edited by
Brigham Young University Press

Library of Congress Cataloging in Publication Data
Main entry under title:

How to involve parents in early childhood
   education.

   Bibliography: At ends of chapters
   1. Education, Preschool—Addresses, essays,
lectures. 2. Parent-teacher relationships—
Addresses, essays, lectures. 3. Parent and
child—Addresses, essays, lectures.
I. Brigham Young University Press.
LB1140.22.H68   1982   372.11'03   82-9468
ISBN 0-8425-2089-9   AACR2

Brigham Young University Press, Provo, Utah 84602

Contents

Introduction

"Parents! Who needs them?" is the lament of many teachers of young children.

- Johnny's parents complain that he doesn't like kindergarten, and they want to know why. Isn't the teacher supposed to *see* that he does?
- Jenny's parents won't come near the school, particularly on parent-teacher conference day. Don't they care about her progress?
- What happens to the notes that accompany the children home from school, inviting parents to attend special events in the classroom? Don't parents know how their absence affects their children?
- Why do Andrea's parents continue to write notes about her psychological problems, as if she were the only child in the class? And why don't they come to the school and discuss the problem in person, as they have been asked to do?
- Who does Mrs. Marler think she is, anyway, telephoning to find fault with the way Jason is responding to classroom prereading exercises? If she thinks she can do any better—!
- Why don't parents pay attention to the assignments sent home with the children and help them complete them? Do they think they have no responsibility in their children's education?

Thus do teachers vent their frustrations, convinced that parents are their nemesis. Either parents interfere too much or they refuse to cooperate. So what to do about parents? Must teachers continue to wish them banished from the earth? Or do viable solutions exist for dealing with them?

1

Perhaps the foregoing examples are exaggerated. Certainly some teachers develop a rapport with their children's parents, and they attest to the efficacy of their successful parent/teacher relationships.

Certainly, too, books have been written on the subject of parenting, including parental involvement in their children's education. Many of these books have been directed toward parents themselves. The sad commentary, however, is that too few parents search out such books and read them.

What many teachers need are ways to reach out and pull parents "in," ways to understand how parents think and feel and ways to help parents understand how teachers think and feel, ways to assure parents they are crucial to their children's lifelong welfare, particularly beginning in the children's early years.

No book can include in its scope the very last word about parent/teacher relationships and parental involvement in early childhood education. This book, however, divides itself into two distinct sections: (1) the historical and present milieu of parental involvement in education and (2) a discussion of how to involve parents in four specific areas of their children's education.

In Part One, Joan E. Herwig ("Parental Involvement: Changing Assumptions about the Educator's Role") reveals that educators were aware of the importance of parental involvement in early childhood education as early as the turn of the century. But because of problems inherent in the attempted liaison of teachers and parents, the move lurched and faltered throughout the succeeding years of this century. Herwig recounts specific reasons for the periodic bogging down of the program. But she insists that parental involvement in the education of their children remains vital to the welfare of those children. Teachers must become as involved in understanding parents and in teaching them their important role in their children's education as they are in teaching the children themselves the rudiments of education. And though teachers must struggle under this dual responsibility, the pay-off in well-adjusted, educated children is worth the effort.

Herwig does not leave the teacher to flounder at this point. She discusses specific problems, such as the psychological effects on both teacher and parent of a close working relationship, and she helps the teacher understand how to deal with the problem. She also discusses plans for classroom activities to be used with parents of differing income levels and suggests the extent to which certain kinds of parents should be expected to become involved.

The conclusion of Herwig's article is that effective parenting in early childhood education enhances the development of both child and parent.

The second article in Part One, "Partnership or Prizefight," by Judith Evans and Lois Bass, deals in greater depth with the psychology of parent-teacher relationships. The authors trace the psychological rift between parents and teachers from its origin to the present day, pointing up the concern of each that the other has attempted—and continues to attempt—to usurp each other's rightful place in the education of children. Thus, the confidence of both parent and teacher is threatened. Solving the problem of distrust between parent and teacher is the burden of this article. A working-together relationship is the solution.

The third article in Part One, "Strategies for a Successful Parental Involvement Program," by Mona S. Johnston, reiterates that most teachers lack understanding of parents' feelings. The author presents graphically some reasons for parents' reluctance to involve themselves, including feelings of anxiety and inadequacy. Johnston's recommendation to teachers is to utilize the best skills and resources of both teacher and parent, developing a mutually supportive partnership for achieving their goals for the children. She outlines principles of effective teacher/parent involvement and includes examples for applying those principles.

The article closing out Part One, by Richard Rundall and Steven Smith: "Working with Difficult Parents," focuses on techniques for teachers who are frustrated about trying to obtain cooperation from unwilling parents. Abusive and neglectful parents, apathetic parents, hostile parents, uneducated parents, critical parents—all these are discussed by Rundall and Smith. Ways of understanding them, then helping them individually to become involved, make up the major portion of the article.

Part Two begins with "Parents and the Child's Search for Self" by Jean Larsen. Educators know that without a healthy self-concept a child cannot learn; thus, including in the curriculum ways of teaching high self-esteem has become commonplace in early childhood education. Because parents spend more time with their children than teachers do, they must learn how to help build their children's positive image of themselves. Larsen describes studies that test various methods of helping parents increase high self-esteem in their youngsters. Teachers of young children may choose among these projects ways to implement a program to help parents.

A second crucial area of education for the young child is reading and, earlier, preparing the child to learn how to read. "Parents and the Reading Process" by Doris Williams emphasizes the importance of parental interest in the prereading/reading process. It also sets forth ways for teachers to involve parents in this most important learning area.

Child's play is another area now recognized as a valuable learning aid for children. In "Parents and Child's Play" Thomas Yawkey presents his International Play Parent-Child Model (YIPPC). His narrative describing the model emphasizes the importance of interaction between parents and children in play and prescribes selected activities to aid teachers in helping parents in this area. Play serves to increase a child's social, academic, and creative growth. When parents understand this concept, they are more willing to encourage their children's play activities.

The fourth article in Part Two, "Parents and the Gifted Child" by Sandra Heater, deals with the early identification of the gifted child and with subsequent plans to tailor that child's schooling to his or her individual needs. The parent is viewed as partner to the teacher in helping in the identification process and in implementing the program set up for the child. Heater suggests at-home activities that teachers may pass along to parents. Most important to the gifted child are parental interest, time, and conversation. These are the elements teachers can help persuade parents to share with their bright offspring.

Thus, although not the last word on parental involvement, this text introduces the subject and recounts its history and the present state of the art. It also presents many helpful concepts and activities to help teachers who wish to include parents in the educative process.

The Education Editor
Brigham Young University

Part 1
The Milieu of Parental Involvement in Early Childhood Education

Parental Involvement:
Changing Assumptions about
the Educator's Role

Joan E. Herwig

Assistant professor of child development at Iowa State University, Dr. Joan E. Herwig teaches child development and parent education courses at both graduate and undergraduate levels. Prior to her present position, she was a public school educator and a consultant for Head Start and daycare centers. She has published articles on child psychology and on the rural family. Currently she is involved in research on play and prosocial behavior in the young child, funded by the Home Economics Research Institute.

Some educators are surprised to learn that the concern for "working with parents" of children in early childhood programs is not a concept solely associated with the 1970s and 1980s. Indeed, as early as 1934 authors were writing on the subject.

> *Parent education is a relatively new movement. Its beginnings in the United States coincide with the rapid rise of the feminist movement, on the one hand, and with the awakening of interest in the social sciences, on the other; its growth has paralleled that of the movements for the scientific study of child development and for progressive education. Today it is an expression of various forces, social, educational and scientific (Staff for the Handbook of Adult Education in the U.S. 1934, p. 8).*

As familiar as the above quote may seem to the contemporary early childhood educator, the historical beginnings of teachers' working with parents, variously referred to as parent education and parental involvement, can be found in early childhood programs in the United States as well as in England at about the turn of the century. For example, the first nursery school, started by Rachel and Margaret McMillan in London in 1908, stressed the importance of working with parents as well as with children. Consequently, teachers visited homes and met with groups of parents to talk about child-rearing techniques. Similarly, kindergartens organized in the United States before the turn of this century tended to schedule the afternoons for teachers to work with parents and to visit homes. Indeed, the Denver public school system initially funded a parent education and preschool program in 1926 that stressed family health education, child-rearing theories, and specific parenting skills (Berger 1981). Bain (1938) states, "The nursery school developed the parent education movement, and from the first embraced the purpose of seeking the coordination of the care and education of young children in the nursery school with the procedures of their homes" (p. 123). The focus on parental involvement was diminished in the 1950s, however, when parents were viewed as unimportant in the teaching process of their children and educators controlled the educational content and delivery of programs. This viewpoint was changed during the 1960s when research findings presented overwhelming evidence that early environment has a profound effect on a child's development (Nedler and McAfee 1979). The 1960s' federally funded Head Start program mandated parental involvement and thus became the first large-scale effort to involve parents in the educational experiences of their children. Other early-childhood programs were stimulated to include parental-involvement activities.

Although the general acknowledgment of the importance of parental involvement by early childhood educators has not changed during this century, the target population, the basic assumptions concerning parental involvement, and the content of parenting advice have changed. The notion of "working with parents," hereafter referred to as parental involvement, directed toward the immigrant and the poor family in the 1920s and 1930s, stressed assimilation into American culture. Middle-class values such as cleanliness, self-discipline and cooperation (Nedler and McAfee 1979) were taught, and child-rearing and home-management advice was given. In contrast, the nursery schools established in the 1920s that were connected with universities typically involved middle-class parents, who were active in parent groups that fostered an interactive process among the university personnel, the parents, and the children (Berger 1981). The parent-cooperative nursery schools, similarly, were organized by middle-class parents who wanted to promote the growth and development of their young children and who attended parent-education groups to discuss new information on child-rearing, guidance, and human development (Nedler and McAfee

1979). It appears that parental-involvement programs serving poor families gave middle-class advice in a didactic, authoritative teacher-to-parent manner with the teacher as the expert, whereas programs serving middle-class families focused on mothers discussing new information.

By the end of the 1950s, general assumptions about early childhood education, according to Nedler and McAfee (1979), included limiting parental involvement to advisory groups, fund-raising and room-mother activities, and membership in the PTA. Public school personnel viewed low-income families as uninterested and ineffective in their children's education. Teachers were the experts working with children, and educators expected children and families to accommodate to the value system of the schools. However, because of the more recent influence of programs such as Head Start, these assumptions can no longer be made. The poor have had greater opportunities to make decisions concerning the educational environment of their children, and a pluralistic view of family values and cultural heritage is reflected in the early childhood curricula and in parental-involvement activities. Now educators recognize that early childhood curricula should be based on the individual needs of the child and the family rather than on institutional or staff priorities. Today parental-involvement activities have expanded to include involving parents in policymaking, helping parents become effective teachers of their own children, allowing parents to provide resources for the school, and helping parents become better-informed persons (Goodson and Hess 1975). A concept of partnership between school and family exists, and attention is focused on the total family rather than solely on the individual child (Berger 1981).

Today the early childhood educator implements a parental-involvement program because she or he believes that what parents do makes a difference in the child's life. The teacher understands that parents have the primary responsibility for rearing children in our society, that parents are the most consistent role models for their child, and that parental attitudes and behaviors influence the child's academic achievement (Nedler and McAfee 1979). Further, the teacher understands the value of parental involvement at a political level—having concern that parents participate in program decision making at an educational level, for parental attitudes toward their children at an interpersonal level, and for creating a sense of community and stability for children (Powell 1978).

Although the early childhood educator acknowledges the vital role of the parent in the child's life and the important role of parental involvement, often the educator experiences frustration in implementing parental-involvement programs. Close examination of the frustrations often indicates several sources of difficulties, such as unrealistic expectations of parents and of early childhood educators, insufficient alternatives for parental-involvement activities, and inadequate knowledge about parental functioning within the early childhood program. Morrison (1978) describes the complexity of educating parents to become involved in their children's educations: "Parent involvement is a process of actualizing the potential of parents; of helping parents discover their strengths, potentialities, and talents; and of using them for the benefit of themselves and the family" (P. 22). Morrison's concept views parents as having talents and skills that can be utilized for the benefit of themselves, their child, and the school. Simultaneously, it recognizes that parents also have many needs that can be met through parental involvement. This definition of parental involvement encompasses a concept extending beyond the notions of teachers providing services *for* parents and parents volunteering their services to the educational program. The parent-teacher interaction is viewed as a *reciprocal* partnership.

We will elaborate here on the pivotal role of early childhood educators in developing in young parents an understanding not only of parent-teacher relationships but also parental involvement. We will present parenting histories, parental-involvement goals, and parental-involvement activity records.

A Developmental Approach to Parental Involvement

Let us consider the parents of young children who have enrolled their firstborn child in an early-childhood program. Where and how do they learn about the parent-teacher relationship? How and when do they learn about expectations and values of parental involvement? Early childhood educators realize the importance of initial educational experiences for children; however, they are not sufficiently aware of the developmental stages of parental involvement.

Several years ago a day-care teacher had an insightful experience concerning parental involvement. It was time for parent-teacher conferences. Parents had scheduled conference times, and the teachers had written anecdotes and prepared materials for the conference. One conference was with Ruth Stace, whose only child, 2½-year-old David, had been enrolled in the classroom for a month. Ruth was in her late twenties and, unlike most day-care parents, had been professionally employed in a position that required considerable contact with parents. She was also a doctoral candidate in the social sciences. Ruth arrived at the conference at the scheduled time, but she was not alone; she came to the conference with two other women! Ruth said, with a mischievous grin, "I hope you don't mind that my mother and grandmother are with me; I am too young to be coming to these parent-teacher conferences by myself!" Although the extended family members were visiting for a holiday and it was coincidental that they were present at the conference, Ruth's comment reveals an acknowledgment of her changing perception of herself as a parent and her inexperience in an unfamiliar role.

This anecdote is familiar to most educators, who recognize statements and nonverbal behavior of parents they have known. They realize they must provide clear information to parents about the value of parental involvement and that they must identify the kinds of parental-involvement activities that will be available during the child's enrollment. They must be supportive of parents as they establish their role with the educator. In other words, educators must assume a more developmental approach to parental involvement. The anecdote reminds teachers they cannot assume that a lack of parental involvement indicates a lack of concern for a child's welfare. It might, instead, represent a lack of knowledge about the responsibility a parent should assume for the child's welfare and a lack of understanding about the ways parental involvement can enhance the child's development.

The early childhood program is an ideal environment for fostering the development of parenting. An early childhood educator is in a pivotal position to influence parental involvement because he or she is the child's first classroom teacher, and this is the first consistent group experience for the child. Thus, parental involvement begins here. The primary task of an early childhood educator is to provide the setting, the experiences, and the guidance that will promote the optimum development of children (Read 1976). A related task is planning parental-involvement activities to help parents grow in confidence and to gain insight and knowledge concerning their child's development.

These educators conduct the first school orientation meeting, greet parents and children daily at the preschool, and schedule the first parent-teacher conference for the young parent whose oldest child is enrolled in his or her first school experience. The early childhood program offers parents an opportunity to examine and to evaluate their own behavior as well as to observe their child. Through classroom observation and interaction, parents can judge whether their techniques and attitudes are as effective as those of others. For example, through observation and communication with the teacher, a father can determine whether his son's biting represents a "stage" that he will eventually grow out of or whether the child is having "problems." Through close parent-teacher interaction this father and his child's teacher can share concerns and satisfactions and can mutually resolve problems and differences for the benefit of both child and adult.

The early childhood educator has a unique opportunity and a responsibility to build a relationship with parents that will enhance communication and will lay a positive, supportive foundation for future parent-teacher relationships. This teaching-learning environment can help young parents broaden their understanding of the interface of home-school communication, and it will facilitate their gradual involvement in parent-teacher activities.

When early childhood educators understand that parents have varying interests, skills, and knowledge about the early childhood program, they approach parental-involvement activities in a more developmental, facilitative way. They give parents more information about the procedures concerning parent-teacher conferences, for example, through newsletter information and personal contacts. They explain specific program goals and activities to parents, and they identify complementary home activities. They respect family interests and cultural heritages, and integrate them into the program planning for children and adults.

Stresses in Parent-Teacher Interaction

Parental development proceeds as parents discuss, observe, participate in, and read about the activities of the early childhood classroom group and, specifically, about their child. However, points of tension develop in the direct exchange between a specific family and the teacher and other staff members with whom they interact (Hess and Croft 1972). Some areas of stress appear to be unavoidable because the family and school have joint responsibility for the child, and both are oriented toward the same child in different ways (see Katz 1980 for further elaboration). Potential sources of stress that result in communication problems include subtle competition between parents and a teacher, a parental viewpoint that considers teachers as potential critics of their success as parents, and a disparity between parents and teacher in cultural background, education, and socioeconomic level.

The wise early childhood educator recognizes that parents might have mixed feelings about their child's attendance at school and might be defensive and uncomfortable in the school situation; therefore, parental-involvement expectations should be individually defined rather than regarded as the same for all parents. The educator should attempt to recognize and value the unique characteristics each parent contributes to his or her parenting situation and to create a parent-teacher relationship that is reassuring, forthright, and constructive.

As social class and ethnicity vary between the parent and the educator, an educator must be very cautious about imposing her value system either on the parent or on the child. Researchers (Laosa 1980, Powell 1977, Winetsky 1978) have found that behavioral expectations for children are influenced by the individual's role, his social class, and his ethnicity. Winetsky (1978) found that the behavioral expectations of most teachers differ from mothers who are non-Anglo or working class or both. Thus, teachers must determine different behavioral expectations of the child in home and at school on such issues as guidance, learning tasks, and classroom membership. This determination might be accomplished initially through specific questions on the family-history enrollment form, such as "When is it necessary to discipline your child?" "What disciplinary measures do you use?" Or a teacher might describe problem situations between an adult and a young child for parents to indicate their preferred solution. As the parent-teacher interaction evolves during the daily arrival and dismissal times and during home visits and parent-teacher conferences, additional similarities and differences in expectations for the child's behavior will become evident. Through this parent-teacher communication, discontinuity between family and school can be reduced for the benefit of all; however, it is unlikely that differences for all families will be eliminated.

Involvement of middle-class and low-income parents presents variable problems. These two groups differ in orientation about school; they do not lack interest in education. Low-income parents often view the teacher as formidable, especially when they have had unfortunate school experiences or limited school achievement. In addition, transportation problems and financial and household-management difficulties might inhibit their participation. In order to plan successful involvement activities for low-income parents, the early childhood educator might find it necessary to provide transportation and child care and to deal with fairly specific practical and concrete issues (Hess and Croft 1972). Specific involvement activities and delivery strategies need modification from those used for middle-class parents, but the general involvement goals remain the same.

Parenting History

Parent-teacher interactions focus on desirable child-rearing behavior through a planned series of experiences that gradually involve the parents with the teacher and, perhaps, the children. Through careful planning the educator can establish preliminary expectations of each parent through parental-involvement activities planned for the classroom. One of the ways this can be accomplished is through either a verbal or written "parenting history" of each parent. Pertinent information would include the family structure (two biological/legal parents, one parent, blended family, dual custody family); number, ages, and types of siblings (step-siblings, half-siblings, foster siblings); members employed (part-time, one parent with one-plus jobs, dual career parents); and the type of employment schedule (shift work, flex-time, split-schedule, substitute, eight-to-five, traveling salesperson, self-employed, on-call). Parental-involvement information requested should include identification of previous parent-education activities (prenatal classes, La Leche League attendance, P.E.T. enrollment, mother's groups); parenting information used (popular magazines, government publications, how-to-parent books); and use of TV programs directed toward parenting ("Footsteps"). Additional information might also include previous parental-involvement activities for older children (P.T.A., open house, parent-teacher conferences, leader of youth organizations such as Scouts or church groups); the address of the noncustodial parent, and preferred parental-involvement activities.

The above information is important to the educator because the family structure indicates *how many* adults can potentially be involved in parenting activities. It also indicates the relationship of the adult to the child. The family employment information indicates *when* the greatest number of parents are available for parenting activities. The parental-involvement history indicates *which* of the parents have already demonstrated an interest in seeking child-rearing information and support. When this information is combined with information regarding the parents' behavioral expectations for a child and is compiled for all families, it is the foundation for planning parental-involvement activities. Some educators will have sufficient knowledge about their children's parents to know they can gather this information directly through a written form, whereas other educators will prefer to get this information during telephone or home contacts.

The emphasis here is on recognizing that many parents have already begun to be "involved parents" through actively seeking child-development knowledge and parent-support groups. Further, it is a recognition that the complexities of family life—its size and structure, its ethnicity and employment demands—are major determinants of the availability of parents for school functions. It is evident that the young mother who is getting a divorce and who has three preschoolers will have different expectations of and availability for parent activities than will the young mother who is a full-time homemaker with an only child and an intact family. And the young father who is a long-distance truck driver has different availability for parenting activities than the young father who is an insurance agent. Similarly, the young Mexican-American mother, the immigrant Indochinese mother, and the black mother differ in their understanding of child-rearing and parent-teacher involvement. As the early childhood educator becomes acquainted with families as unique units, she will recognize the dynamic pluralistic nature of contemporary parents and family life. Consequently, the planned parent goals and activities will be more realistic, constructive, and varied.

Setting Parental-Involvement Goals

When the early childhood educator has begun to understand her students' parents, she must decide what skills and attitudes she should foster in them; then, she must implement a program of educating them.

She does this with an awareness that parents are not static, rigid entities. Her plans for parental involvement will vary as parents change in their interactions with the school and as the classroom group changes. Ideally, these experiences should evolve from passive listening on the part of parents to eager discussion and to active use of the information in a realistic situation (Todd and Heffernan 1977), although some parents will continue to prefer a significant social distance from the early childhood program and its staff (Powell 1977).

The goals should be based upon the interests and skills of the parent, upon the parent's expressed preference, and upon the teacher's parenting skills. Some parents will be eager to be involved in the classroom as soon as the teacher can schedule the activity, whereas others will be more reluctant, or even unwilling, to be involved. Some parents might want to hear about the experiences of other parents' involvement before determining their own involvement. For the very reluctant parent, a teacher should delay scheduling a classroom activity. It might be preferable for the teacher to begin by encouraging an increase in the parent's observation time at arrival and dismissal times without labeling it an involvement activity. As Powell (1977) reports, teachers should recognize that some parents will have a low frequency of communication with educators, will enter into almost no discussion of parent/family-related topics, and will maintain an attitude that child-rearing values and family information should not be discussed with educators. These parents do not perceive the early childhood center as a child-rearing or child-development information source, and they are not likely to adopt a pattern of parental involvement in the early childhood program.

The selection of an appropriate activity might be facilitated by having parents indicate on a record form specific family interests they may be willing to share at school. A checklist of family interests might include arts and crafts, cooking, musical instruments, carpentry, travel experiences, ethnic heritage, occupation-related skills, and pets. The willingness of parents to share their skills with children also might be identified on a checklist including such things as field-trip driver, equipment construction and maintenance, classroom resource person, story-reader or storyteller, special-food cook, special projects, and home-resource provider. Further, parents could indicate on this form their preferences for other parental-involvement activities, such as participating in parent-teacher conferences or becoming a Parent-Policy Board member; joining study groups or attending specifically listed special events and programs; welcoming home visits; and taking part in classroom observation. Since teachers often learn about additional family talents and interests through informal contacts and home visits, the checklist should be considered an initial source of information rather than a complete indication of the parent's interests and preferences.

Although teachers might think of many suitable parental-involvement goals, Read and Patterson (1980) indicate two major goals for teachers working with parents: to help parents gain confidence and to help parents obtain a better understanding about children and their needs. The first goal might be accomplished through informal contacts with each parent, newsletter recognition of a parent's contributions, the provision of a "parent area" (a room, a bulletin board) and through clearly expressed teacher expectations of the parent. The second goal would be more specifically stated to address developmental topics, such as the value of play and play activities for young children with emphasis on provisions for touching, exploring, and manipulating. This goal might be reached through classroom observation followed by discussion, recommended books or articles, newsletters and informal contacts, and parent discussion groups.

The educator might begin by selecting a goal to involve each parent with classroom activities on an individual, predetermined basis. That goal might be initially implemented by having Parent A observe specific classroom activities, Parent B talk about his work as a shoe salesperson, and Parent C make applesauce with a few children. Parent B might participate during the fourth week of school, Parent C the eighth week, and Parent A the ninth week. Following the participation of each parent, the teacher and parent should take a few minutes to share their individual observations and questions about the children's behaviors and skills. In addition, the information concerning desirable methods of work with children should be related to each parent's family situation. Remember that the ultimate goals are to make parents feel at ease in their role as parents, to increase their understanding of children, to facilitate home-school communication by reducing the fragmentation and discontinuity of child-rearing practices and to coordinate the child's socialization processes.

Parental-Involvement Record Keeping

As individual goals for parents evolve, teachers will find helpful maintaining records concerning parents' involvement. Such records will be most beneficial if 1) the teacher devises her own workable format, 2) keeps the records in a convenient place for easy record entry and 3) uses the records to determine future parental-activity plans by noting progress. The records serve as documentation of parental activity for early childhood center annual reports as well as a statement of progress for each parent and an evaluation of the types of parental involvement. For example, the September–December record of Parent A may reflect a change in involvement from passive to active (from attendance at Orientation Night to donating materials for the woodworking center to monthly classroom participation during lunch hour). The record should also describe the parent's involvement and should reflect the educator's contact with the parent (notes, phone calls, home visits). Although the parental-activity record serves as a formal record designed to enhance the development of parental involvement, it should not inhibit the valuable informal interactions that occur at school or in the community. It is advisable not to circulate the records for use beyond the classroom, and these records should be maintained separately from the child's records.

Parental-Involvement Activities

Parental-involvement activities have been categorized in several ways. Powell (1977) uses sources of parent-teacher communication; Schickedanz (1977) defines levels of parental involvement; and Filipczak (1977) identifies four types of parental-involvement activities. Each of these authors acknowledges the variety of parental-involvement activities that reflect the quality of parent-teacher interactions. (Schickedanz defines involvement according to the degree the role of teacher as "expert" and school personnel as "decision makers" are altered.) Thus, parental-involvement activities offer a variety of commitments from parents and teachers.

Individual parent conferences, parent meetings for the purpose of social events or orientation, provision of snacks and donation of "junk" materials for classroom use are examples of important parental-involvement activities that do not challenge the expertise of the teacher or the decision-making power of the school. Many parents will quite readily participate in these activities. But activities requiring parental presence and participation in the educational setting, such as parent visitation, observation, and classroom volunteering, demand a different level of commitment and self-confidence of both the parent and the teacher. The parent-teacher interaction is actively shared. The most demanding level of parental involvement is characterized by activities that involve parents in teaching their own children and in making decisions concerning educational policy (Schickedanz 1977). As members of school policy councils and as participants at parent workshops designed to teach parent-child activities for home or school use, parents are demonstrating a high level of commitment and self-confidence.

Early childhood educators who understand that the amount of self-esteem varies in parents as do their understanding and commitment to parental-involvement activities will plan for a variety of activities that enable all kinds of parents to participate. That is, the teacher will not expect all parents to become policy board members or to volunteer in the classroom.

Early childhood educators can plan for parental-involvement activities much as they plan curriculum for young children. That is, at the beginning of the academic year the teacher roughly "plots out" the types of parental-involvement activities she will organize and will establish time lines for implementing the activities. Then as the year progresses, the teacher determines the specific content of the activity based upon parental interest, resources available, and expressed needs. For example, prior to the beginning of the program year, the teacher decides if and, generally when, she will schedule newsletters, meetings, orientations, conferences and observations. Later, as the approximate date approaches, she determines whether to implement the activity and, if so, what content to include. Preplanning serves as a guideline and an overview of parental-involvement activities that complement information about the parents themselves, including parental-involvement goals and parent history. Preplanning also removes some of the confusion involved—the "it's-the-end-of-the-month-so-I-should-write-a-newsletter" dilemma.

What are some possible parental-involvement activities? What are the purposes and structures of parental-involvement activities? How can these activities be adapted to serve parents who have a variety of developmental parenting skills? These questions and others will be answered in the following section. Specific parental-involvement activities will be considered by highlighting the way each activity can foster the parents' understanding as well as their involvement.

These activities represent the types of strategies a teacher would use to implement an active parental-involvement program. These activities, selected by the teacher, would be recorded on the parental-involvement log for each parent or family. In addition, the teacher would have to make some provision in the log for recording more spontaneous activities.

Preadmission Orientation. The initial parent-teacher communication marks the beginning of the home-school interaction, whether the contact is by telephone or in person. Discussion about the child, the program, and the staff should also include consideration of parental-involvement expectations and activities. When the parent tours the school facilities, parent bulletin boards, the parent library, and other indications of parental involvement should be highlighted. Perhaps the latest parent newsletter could be included in the admissions materials. The primary goals at this time are to respond to parents in a human way and to show interest in them. Additional involvement goals are to portray an expectation that parental involvement is an integral part of the early childhood program and that involvement activities are diverse.

Orientation Meeting. Typically the purpose of the orientation meeting is to review school policies, complete admissions records, establish enrollment procedures (that is, gradual enrollment) and serve as the initial planned parent activity. The staff should review planned involvement activities, such as parent-teacher conferences, parent-policy board meetings, parent education meetings and newsletters, and more informal contacts. This meeting will also reveal the location of parent services, such as the parent bulletin board and the parent resource library and observation area, if available. Parents may find it reassuring to know how the "parent history" (the checklist of family interest, the checklist of preferred parental-involvement, and related information) will be used. This meeting is a vehicle to establish a community of people—parents and staff—who are willing to become involved with one another for the mutual benefit of children, families, and staff.

Arrival and Dismissal Time. If parents regularly drop off and pick up their children, this provides a set time for a substantive exchange of child- and family-related issues. This exchange is the most potent and frequent form of parental-involvement activity (Wolfe 1981). Because of this meeting's frequency and informal, spontaneous nature, here the initial "hello" can be extended to include more child-, parent-, and family-related topics. During this parent-teacher interaction parents often share their personal family/parenting concerns. The parent who asks, "How can I get Lee to bed earlier at night?" or "Roberto has problems sharing at home. Is that also true at school?" or "Why don't you have coloring books here?" is seeking substantive answers. That is a "teachable moment." The wise teacher will respond sincerely with accurate information and, depending on the parent's response, may offer additional reading material and related information. Or she may follow up later with an inquiry about the current status concerning the question.

The frequency and quality of parent-teacher interaction during these times depend upon the availability of the teacher, the location of the transition place, and the atmosphere created by the teacher and the staff. Early childhood educators need to scrutinize the parent activity. Is furniture arranged that parents may have easy access to the teacher? Is a teacher regularly available to greet parents and children? Does the teacher always seem to communicate with the same parents or with staff members during this time? Does the teacher initiate interesting, nonthreatening conversation, or does she expect parents to be the only initiators?

Some teachers may want to keep a tally of their interactions for a short time to evaluate their performance. A tally form indicating the number of parents spoken to, the approximate length of contact, and the topic discussed may be suitable for self-evaluation.

While respecting individual interaction patterns, the goals of this activity are to establish trust between parent and teacher, to provide a consistent time for discussion of child-parent-family topics and to coordinate the child's socialization process. The perceptive teacher will become aware that some parents are more verbal at arrival versus dismissal time, that some parents prefer to discuss only child-related topics, and that some parents prefer relating to a specific staff member.

Parent Bulletin Boards and Displays. Teachers often consider the development of parent bulletin boards and displays time-consuming and of little value. Consequently, they often are a low priority in a teacher's demanding schedule. However, they may have greater value than teachers recognize. Powell (1977) found that "independent parents," who are characterized by a low frequency of communications with staff members, utilize nonstaff sources of communication (such as a bulletin board) as the main channel of communication with the center. This suggests that within every group of parents some of them would rely on bulletin boards and displays for parent-school information.

For bulletin boards to be useful however, they must be visible and attractive. Is the bulletin board in your center located in a well-lit and accessible place for parent use? Are the displayed materials appealing, legible, relevant, and interesting? Is the reading level appropriate for your parents? Are "take-away" materials occasionally provided for parents to use elsewhere? How often is the material changed?

Appropriate topics for the bulletin board could include developmental and health information, activities for children and families, child advocacy and child care issues, and announcements of center and community events. Teachers may want to develop their own materials, but suitable materials are available from the local Cooperative Extension Office. Some teachers like to coordinate display content for parents with the children's programming, and to use parent and child photographs taken at the center to increase parents' attention to the bulletin board. The bulletin board could also be coordinated with the newsletter, thus: "For further information see the parent bulletin board." Or "Use the bulletin board to schedule parent-teacher conference." Display content could be planned sequentially for several weeks rather than as discontinuous, isolated topics. For example, the topic of pre-reading skills in the preschool might evolve over several weeks with a consecutive display of pertinent book jackets, Cooperative Extension handouts on children's cognitive ability, and photos of children using assorted prereading materials.

Bulletin boards and displays serve as the primary source of information for some parents, provide supplementary information to all parents, and are a vital link in home-school involvement. This avenue of communication is respectful of parents who prefer indirect contact with the school.

Newsletters. A common form of indirect, or nonstaff, source of information to parents is the newsletter. The newsletter is a short, practical form of newspaper written for a selected audience. It is either representative of a specific classroom, a grade level, or an entire early childhood program. Similar to the use of parent bulletin boards and displays, newsletters serve as a main channel of communication between the center and "independent parents" (Powell 1977). Newsletters, therefore, are a vital source of information for some parents. In addition they can be distributed to other interested community members, such as the Board of Directors, center sponsors, supportive community leaders, and prospective parents.

Whether the newsletter is multipage typeset or one-page mimeographed, similar expectations of production quality and relevant content remain. Does the newsletter heading clearly identify the address and telephone number of the center, the name of the director/ teacher/principal, and the date? Is the newsletter legible and attractive? Does the content and appearance represent planning and careful selection, or is it haphazard and cluttered? Is the content written in an interesting, informative manner appropriate to the reading level of the readers? Does the newsletter distribution procedure ensure its reaching the intended reader?

Newsletter content may include center and community announcements, early childhood program content and activities information, school policies such as health and safety, a schedule of events, and parent education information. The content of one issue might be devoted to an upcoming event. For example, a newsletter preceding the parent conference might explain the purpose of the conference, what the parent and teacher should learn at the conference, the scheduling and format of a conference, and conference topics. Newsletters are also ideal places to present developmental information. Perhaps several sequential newsletters could present child-development information on such topics as language or social development or on the value of outdoor play. Children's anecdotes from the classroom, recognition of specific parental involvement, and announcements of family events such as children's birthdays, birth or adoption of siblings, and enrollment of new children are always interesting to parents.

If the teacher selects articles about individual children or families, she should be sure to include every child or family within a short period of time. Recording the newsletter date on the parental-involvement form will help the teacher quickly determine which children or families have not been cited in a newsletter. Record keeping is important to avoid creating communication barriers and accusations of preferential treatment.

Distribution of the newsletter is important, also. It is advisable for each child enrolled, including siblings, to get a copy of the newsletter to take home, so they don't feel neglected or overlooked.

Telephone conversations, notes, letters, happy-grams. These devices for communication tend to be family-specific and spontaneous, and they address a significant occurrence, such as Elizabeth's success at dressing herself or Antonio's unsolicited helpful assistance or the formation of a new friendship by Julio and Michael. They might be a response to a parent's question or request, or a mutual concern.

Again, it is important to keep records of the date each contact is made, that the educator may evaluate the frequency and number of families contacted. Even young children become aware of the "special letters" that are being sent to selected homes. A kindergarten teacher in a midwestern community sent a happy-gram each Friday to the child who demonstrated the best behavior in the class during that week. The goal was a sincere effort to praise children and to communicate with parents. However, the children were becoming physically and emotionally upset on Fridays. With twenty-five children in the classroom, some child had to wait longer than six months to receive the highly prized happy-gram! While the intent of happy-grams is commendable, the selection criteria for distribution must be appropriate to the child's age. Can five-year-olds reasonably wait six or even five months before they receive special recognition?

Any of these forms of communication requires a concerted effort by the sender to convey a spirit of spontaneous sincerity (Berger 1981). Good communication, either written or verbal, is preserved by sincerity and messages that have meaning. Stiff, contrived communication probably will be detected by the parents. The goal of these forms of communication is to communicate spontaneously with parents in a positive manner that will improve parent-teacher relations and the child's self-concept.

Parent observations. Parents should be encouraged to observe the early childhood program as the year progresses. The observation can be more successful if the parent is prepared in advance. Parents will want to have procedural information (arrival time, where to sit, how to react to the child) as well as content suggestions (what to look for) and communication information (when to talk with the teacher and staff). Procedural information could be provided via the newsletter or by personal contact. Content suggestions depend upon the reason the parent is visiting and the schedule of activities when the parent is present. Adjustments in scheduling may be necessary to accommodate the need for parental observation. The teacher will have to plan her time in order to greet the parent and discuss the observation with the parent before he or she leaves. Perhaps the teacher will have to provide child-care arrangements, either in the classroom or elsewhere, for preschool siblings so that parents and babysitters can visit the early childhood program in session.

Some teachers provide classroom visitors, including parents, with an "observation letter" when they arrive at the classroom for routine visits. It greets parents, suggests procedural guidelines, and offers observation recommendations. For example, one teacher uses a question format to guide parent observations by asking, among other things, "How do the children respond to one another? What examples of sharing, cooperation and difficult behavior do you see? How are children's questions answered? How does the teacher use the children's ideas and interest?" By using questions, she guides the parent's observations to room environment, guidance, curriculum, and classroom management without using technical, often foreboding, terms.

The purposes of observation are to communicate that the parent is welcome in the classroom, to assist the parent in understanding the early childhood program as a basis for coordinating the child's socialization process, to determine a way he or she might become involved in the classroom, and to model teaching techniques that the parent might find applicable to his or her parent-child relationship. These goals can be met best when the teacher provides discussion time during the parent's classroom observation. Communication about particular activities, children's behavior, and classroom rules and routines can clarify any misunderstandings or misinterpretations that might occur. Further, explicit explanations help parents comprehend the sometimes vague and abstract relationship between child development and early childhood education programming. Through careful questioning the teacher can determine similarities and differences in the socialization process between home and school; then initial efforts to reduce any discontinuity can begin.

Parent-Teacher Conferences. The parent conference is a good opportunity for a parent and a teacher to discuss an individual child in a personal, face-to-face situation and to share their understanding of the child with the intent of determining ways to facilitate the child's development. Although conferences are time consuming, their benefits overshadow the time factor. Parents and teachers view the parent conference as an excellent opportunity for clarifying issues, searching for answers, deciding on goals, determining mutual strategies, and forming a team for the child's education (Berger 1981).

There are many purposes, relating to the needs of the child, for conducting parent conferences. The conferences might be planned for the second or third week of enrollment and used to assess the child's general adjustment to school. A mutual assessment of the child's progress and developmental abilities could be used to develop a specific plan for home-school interaction. Other purposes might be to identify the parent's goals, feelings, and expectations for the child or to determine how the values and beliefs of the school interface with those of the home. A clear statement of the purpose for the conference allows the teacher to establish criteria not only for assessing the conference's success but also for creating guidelines for conference planning. It also helps parents prepare for the conference and feel more at ease during its progression.

Conferences can be a better source of communication if both parents have had preparation. The invitation to attend the conference sets the tone. A cordial invitation that recognizes the parent's busy schedule and many responsibilities by providing options for scheduling conferences is an important factor. For example, in addition to the common afternoon times, evening, morning, and lunch hour conferences may need to be scheduled to accommodate for parents working unusual hours or to encourage both parents to attend.

Information presented in a newsletter or on a parent bulletin board and in special letters also help prepare parents for conferences. A newsletter, distributed several weeks before conferences begin and perhaps before the invitations are sent could be devoted to parent conference expectations, structure, and content. This information helps reduce parents' anxiety because it gives them time to prepare for the conference. Consequently, the conference can be devoted to a sincere exchange concerning the child because parents have had time to think about their child's development and progress. Adequate preparation helps parents realize that sharing information about the child can assist the process of determining goals and strategies to help the child. Information on the parent bulletin board also could reinforce the parent-conference newsletter information.

A note should be sent to each family confirming the time, the date, and the exact location of the conference. Either a form letter or a personal note from the teacher can be used. The note could remind parents of the newsletter and parent bulletin-board suggestions.

Preconference preparation for the teacher includes providing parents with information, scheduling choices, and organizing materials denoting pupil progress. The teacher should review and analyze a child's previous records, his current performance and attitude, and his relationships with peers and adults. Anecdotal records, art projects, and other paperwork should be collected throughout the child's enrollment. This work is an important assessment tool.

During the conference, parents should be asked to tell about their child's likes and dislikes, his response to the early childhood program, activities outside the program, problems that may be occurring, and specific help needed. The teacher should describe the child's typical behavior patterns, his interests, and his social relationships, noting any unusual development. Classroom activities and the class schedule should be discussed also. The teacher should use simple, clear language so that parents are not confused by phrases like *eye-hand coordination, dyad interactions, ITA,* and *Peabody materials.* She or he should be straightforward and honest throughout the conference, even when problems such as guidance, differences in cultural values and interpretations, and the child's immature development must be confronted.

Some points to consider in planning parent-teacher conferences include the following: Is the conference held in a quiet place away from interruptions and distractions? Is the seating space and room arranged to aid informality and communication? Does the teacher ask parents for their opinions and observations; then does she listen attentively? Does the teacher use familiar terminology instead of specialized, technical language? Does the conference end with mutual goals and strategies to help the child and with a plan for future conversations to determine progress? Does the teacher speak 50 percent or less of the time during the conference? Does the teacher present accurate information about the child, including problem behaviors or attitudes?

After the conference is over, the teacher should make careful records of the conference for later personal reference. Discussion highlights, suggestions, follow-up activities, and a timeline for future conversations should be recorded. Sometimes follow-up referrals to other resource people will be necessary.

The parent conference is one of the most effective methods for a teacher to have two-way communication with parents. An informal study by Berger (1981) indicated that parents view the parent-teacher conference as their most important opportunity for communicating with their child's teacher. Although conferences are accepted by most parents as a valuable part of parental involvement, not all parents will attend a conference. Powell (1977) found that 25 percent of a day-care parent sampling never attended a conference. When parents do not attend conferences, the teacher must review possible explanations for their nonattendance. Issues such as personal or family problems, conference information provided and procedures followed, and previous contacts with the family must be considered. Perhaps attendance might be increased by offering other conference dates and another location, or perhaps a greater number of personal notes reassuring the parent about the child's progress would be helpful.

All in all, 100 percent attendance at conference is the exception rather than the rule. However, the teacher must keep trying new strategies to increase parent participation. Whatever its frequency, the child should not suffer repercussions from the teacher for the parents' choices and behaviors. For example, competition among classrooms for total parent-conference attendance is especially unfair if conferences are scheduled only during the day when parents work or if children are living in single-parent families and only one parent can attend. Nonattendance at parent conferences is not necessarily rejection of the child or the teacher. It can be a reflection of cultural or socioeconomic values, of pressures and stress, and of work demands.

When the conference is viewed as another form of parental involvement, when a substantial amount of preconference planning has taken place, communication can be open and honest; interaction is less anxious and defensive. Teacher and parent alike can find invaluable opportunities to share and exchange information, each one then assuming responsibilities for meeting the child's needs. The teacher must set realistic expectations, both for parents and herself, in determining the success of the conferences. Some progress, some frustration, and a continuing demand for new solutions to contemporary needs are logical and natural outcomes from these sessions.

Parent meetings. Parental involvement in the form of parent meetings or group discussion has many purposes and structures. These discussions can be organized either by the teacher or by the parents. They may be quite formal, programmed to present a commercial parent education program such as STEP, or informal, featuring coffee hours or work sessions. The meetings might be primarily social events, fostering group participation or educational opportunities or a blend of both.

No matter what the content or who organizes the parent meetings, the primary ingredient is parent interest. The meetings provide parents an opportunity for contact with other parents to share both the concerns and the interest they are experiencing. The common factor among the parents is that they have children of the same age and at the same stage of development. Further, since their children are enrolled in an early childhood program, the parents have common experiences as their children increase in independence and in developing friendships.

Sometimes topics for group discussions evolve from informal suggestions by parents; at other times teachers conduct a more formal needs assessment. Typically, a needs assessment lists possible meeting times and dates and various topics for parents to indicate their preferences. From these responses, parent meetings are planned that will appeal to the greatest number of parents. In a large early childhood program, several parent meetings are offered simultaneously.

Some teachers have found that parents are reluctant, especially at the beginning of the school year, to commit themselves to active participation in parent meetings. Therefore, teachers begin the school year by planning other types of parent group activities. Such things as a Saturday work day to paint equipment or build outdoor play equipment, a family potluck picnic, or an afternoon work session to make puzzles and games or to repair library books help parents to become acquainted and to informally share their time and skills for their child's benefit. A Head Start teacher wisely scheduled work sessions early in September to make children's games. As the mothers assembled the games, they shared many topics of mutual interest, including child-rearing, household management, and personal interests; and the women began to identify their common interests and concerns. The teacher mentally recorded these topics and, after several afternoon work sessions, suggested they continue to meet to discuss in greater detail some of the previously mentioned topics. The mothers, comfortable in this new setting, proud of their work efforts, and eager to continue their new friendships, willingly agreed to the meetings and eventually began assuming responsibility for the meetings. In this situation the teacher avoided using the rather foreboding terms *parent meeting* or *parent education*; and she avoided scheduling meetings on topics such as discipline, child nutrition, and health and safety hazards around the home until the parents were comfortable with the school setting and with each other. Further, by attending to some of the mothers' personal needs, such as security, acceptance, and a nonjudgmental attitude as part of the parent discussion programming, the teacher established a good rapport with them. Low-key work sessions, a crafts class, exercise groups, or coffee hours are less foreboding and inhibiting to many parents, and, consequently, they are effective ways to begin and to maintain parent interest when they are combined with other, more traditional topics of parent meetings.

The success of a parent meeting can be enhanced by attention to pertinent concerns. Have you asked parents about desirable meeting times and topics of interest? Have you planned meetings that appeal directly to the parents' self-development as well as to their child-rearing role? Are the meetings periodically evaluated to determine if they are continuing to meet parents' needs and interests? Do parents share responsibility for the meetings?

During the discussion many particular problems are often presented that require a moderator or leader. Often the teacher, especially in the beginning, must relate the examples to general principles or to group interests. Parents might be asked to present at the meeting a typical example of a child's behavior or of parent-child interaction to stimulate further discussion. Typically, group meetings do not last beyond an hour and a half, although some participants may continue to talk informally after the meeting.

Parent meetings are an important strategy for parental involvement that extends and supplements the exchange of home-school information from parent conferences and from arrival and dismissal time. They are a continuing program that must change in content and structure as group interests change during the year. Teachers are necessary for assessing group interests, helping establish group rapport and commitment, and locating resources.

Home visits. Although most parental-involvement activities occur in the early childhood center other desirable activities should be planned for other settings such as parks for family potluck picnics and the parents' homes for home visits. Center-based early childhood programs schedule home visits for various reasons during the year, including visits prior to the child's enrollment to become acquainted with the child and his family and, later in the year, to see the child functioning in his home and to share mutual topics of interest. The teacher might also make brief home visits when the child has been ill for several days. Teachers sometimes take materials (puzzles, paper, and crayons) for the child and his siblings to use during the visit. The "new" activity usually helps the children direct their excitement and pleasure to constructive activities, which in turn help the parents relax and feel more comfortable with the teacher.

Home visits for center-based programs are primarily social occasions for the teacher and the family to become better acquainted on the parents' "turf." Advance preparation about the purposes of the home visits, such as discussing these purposes at the Orientation Meeting or pointing them out in the Parent Handbook or a newsletter, and adequate early scheduling of the home visit help reduce parents' concerns about home visits. Typically, home visits are a new experience for the family; parents want to know why the teacher is visiting the home. Is it an inspection of the home and family? Should we houseclean before the visit to make sure we "pass inspection"? Do we have to invite the teacher to dinner, too? Why don't we meet at the early childhood center instead of at our home?

Since home visits may be anxiety producing for the parents, the first visit should be brief and should emphasize the child's successes in school and the special qualities the child possesses. Of course, the teacher should stress her sincere interest in the family throughout the visit and should emphasize the similarities of their life experiences, empathizing with the family's situation and highlighting family strengths rather than their differences and limitations. The home visit, generally, is neither the time nor the place to discuss the child's specific problems because privacy is usually not available. If a specific problem is mentioned and pursued by the parent, however, it is appropriate for the teacher to express concern for the child and the family and to offer assistance in discussing the problem with the parent at a mutually agreed upon time and place.

Teachers might want to coordinate home visits with classroom activities or parent meetings. For example, a parent meeting could be planned for the parent who expresses an interest in learning about home educational activities, and that meeting could be followed by scheduled home visits. These visits could be used to see how the parent and the child are using selected materials (materials made at the parent meeting), and to discuss other ways to use available equipment and materials in the home. Photographs of the child's pet or of his family could be taken, later to be used at school. The purpose of this visit would be to devise mutual activities for use at home and school that utilize and respect the resources of both environments.

Occasionally parents will express no interest or even open hostility toward a teacher's requests for home visits. When this happens, a teacher should approach parental involvement more slowly and should focus on other less threatening parent-teacher activities, such as news-letters, personal notes, arrival and dismissal contact, and parent dis-cussions. Continued contact with the teacher and feedback from other parents who have had home visits may help the reticent parents be-come more accepting of the teacher's intentions and purposes for the home visits.

Home visits for center-based programs serve several purposes, but they are always occasions for the teacher to demonstrate interest in the child and in the family. They are offered as a parental-involvement ac-tivity to decrease the discontinuity between home and school through face-to-face dialogue between parent and teacher.

Additional parental-involvement activities. Other types of parent-school communication include telephone conferences and special-events programs. Programs that avoid holidays help reduce expectations on parents' busy schedules. Family night, a school carnival, and an art show of the children's work throughout the year are examples of events that have been successful in many early childhood programs.

In addition to parent observations, some parents may want to be more involved within the early childhood program. Common opportu-nities for this type of activity include a parent becoming an assistant to the teacher (cooking with the children or reading to them), being a speaker (bringing a family pet or a collection of stones, seashells, or miniatures to share and talk about at school), being a performer (singing or playing a musical instrument) and being a field-trip driver. Partici-pating on parent-policy boards and being a home resource provider bringing empty food containers, fabric and yarn scraps, clothes for make-believe) also represent valuable volunteer activities although they demand highly diverse levels of participation and commitment.

Parent-education activities can evolve from parent meetings. A par-ent lending library containing magazines (such as *Parents Magazine* and *Working Mothers*), books and pamphlets with varied reading levels and topics, and teacher-prepared bibliographies on selected topics may be the basis for several parent meetings or study groups. They may even be preferred by the "independent parent." More structured parent-education programs, such as STEP (Systematic Training for Effective Parenting) or the Dreikurs program, both requiring a commitment of several weeks, are possibilities also.

It is not necessary for early childhood educators to provide all of the parental-involvement activities. Many communities offer a variety of opportunities to parents through the Cooperative Extension Service, public health offices, the public library, churches, and other agencies. The teacher can serve as a clearinghouse and can provide "public ser-vice announcements" by informing parents, through the newsletter or the bulletin board, about current parent-education events. The teacher can arrange to attend the events with a group of interested parents.

Conclusion

The early childhood educator has a crucial and pivotal responsibility to establish the foundation of parental involvement in the responsibility of caring for children. Although many parental-involvement activities are available for the early childhood educator's selection, successful parenting activities require a teacher's keen understanding of her classroom parents. Family structure, employment schedules, previous parental involvement, current interests, and cultural and educational backgrounds are vital factors influencing the success of activities for parents. Programs that reflect an understanding and an appreciation of the parents' backgrounds and that assist them in understanding the why and how of parental involvement will help parents become more involved in the early childhood program. Programs that communicate a "can do" attitude and provide a variety of parental-involvement activities while respecting parents as individuals will create home and school environments that are conducive to the development not only of children but also of adults.

References

Bain, W. 1938. Problems of home-school relationships in nursery school and kindergarten. *Parent Education* 4: 123–27.

Berger, E. H. 1981. *Parents as partners in education.* St. Louis: The C. V. Mosby Co.

Filipczak, J. 1977. *Parental involvement in the schools: towards what end?* Silver Spring, Maryland: Institute for Behavioral Research (ERIC-ECE Document).

Goodson, B., and Hess, R. 1975. *Parents as teachers of young children: an evaluative review of some contemporary concepts and programs.* Stanford, Calif.: Stanford University Press.

Katz, L. G. 1980. Mothering and teacher—some significant distinctions. In *Current topics in early childhood education,* vol. 3, ed. Lillian G. Katz, pp. 47–63. Norwood, New Jersey: ABLEX Publishing Corporation.

Kroth, R. L., and Simpson, R. L. 1977. *Parent conferences as a teaching strategy.* Denver, Colorado: Love Publishing Co.

Laosa, L. M. 1980. Maternal teaching strategies in Chicano and Anglo-American families: the influence of culture and education on maternal behavior. *Child Development* 51.

Morrison, C. S. 1978. *Parent involvement in the home, school and community.* Columbus: Charles E. Merrill Publishing Company.

Nedler, S. E., and McAfee, O. D. 1979. *Working with parents.* Belmont, California: Wadsworth.

Powell, D. R. 1977. *The interface between families and child care programs: a study of parent-caregiver relationships.* The Merrill-Palmer Institute.

Read, K. H. 1976. *The nursery school.* 6th ed. Philadelphia: W. B. Saunders Company.

Schickedanz, J. A. 1977. Parents, teachers and early education. In *Early Childhood Education*, eds. Leonard H. Golubchick and Barry Persky, pp. 331–33. Wayne, New Jersey: Avery Publishing Group.

Staff for the *Handbook of adult education in the United States.* 1934. Parent Education in the United States, *Parent Education* 1: 8–9, 31.

Todd, V. E., and Heffernan, H. 1977. *The years before school: guiding preschool children.* 3rd ed. New York: MacMillan Publishing Co.

Winetsky, C. 1978. Comparisons of the expectations of parents and teachers for the behavior of preschool children. *Child Development* 49: 1146–54.

Wolfe, C. 1981. Communication patterns between parents and providers in family day care settings. Master's thesis, Iowa State University.

Parental Involvement:
Partnership or Prizefight?

Judith L. Evans and Lois Bass

Judith L. Evans, Ed.D., is well qualified to coauthor an article on the psychology of parent-teacher relationships. Her educational background includes developmental and educational psychology, and her professional career has expanded upon these areas. She has done research in childhood learning in Cali, Colombia, and in East African countries; she has studied the effects of mother-child interaction on child development; and she is at present director of the Parent-Infant Department at the High/Scope Educational Research Foundation in Ypsilanti, Michigan. Dr. Evans is President of the Michigan Association for Infant Mental Health.

Lois Bass, with an educational background in family counseling and social services, has worked as a counselor-therapist responsible for ameliorating a variety of social problems, including drug dependency, single parenting, and marital incompatibility. As a school social worker, she has worked with families and parent groups, especially emphasizing handicapped infants and toddlers.

> *Nothing is worse than interfering parents. Over the years I have found that the best way to handle them is to invite them as a group into the classroom early in the year and tell them what I will be doing. That always satisfies them. They won't bother me all year long if I placate them early on.*
>
> *—A teacher.*

I am the parent of four children. I wear two hats in relationship to the public schools—one as a professional educator and another as a parent whose children are in the school system. I have as much or more education as the professionals working with my child. I am as middle class as they are, and I certainly know my way around the public school system because I have been a resident of the city for twenty-seven years. But I still feel cowed when I go to the conference. I feel guilty because my child is sometimes very disturbing in school and I feel that I am a bad parent. I get nervous, angry, defensive, aggressive, and apologetic.

—A parent.

Parents and Teachers at Odds

Throughout a child's early school experience the key people in that child's life often fail to get together to talk about the child's experiences, to learn from one another, or to design ways each of them can support the child's learning. These key people are the child's parents and teachers. Each, in his or her own way, is anxious to do the best possible for the child. Yet each tends to operate at odds with the other. Why? What does this mean for the child? What does it mean for parents and teachers?

In this article we explore the historical development of the gap between home and school and the evolution of the concept of parental involvement—what it has come to mean and how it needs to be expanded in the best interests of the children. Several explanations exist for the rift between teachers and parents. One is provided by a brief review of the history of education in this country.

Teachers as Socializers

When schools first opened their doors in the United States, they were an extension of the home—espousing the same values, beliefs, and goals as the families they served. In time, however, particularly in more urban areas containing a variety of immigrant groups, schools assumed an important socialization role: they provided a place where youngsters from a variety of ethnic backgrounds could be brought together and could be "Americanized." Our country was a "melting pot," where nationalities were set aside for a common good. The role schools played in this socialization process was supported and applauded by parents, who were anxious that their children become "American" as soon as possible. The school had a clear function in the melting-pot society: to educate the children to fit into the broader society, while the home provided the wider base of support for the child's growth and development.

Although the melting pot notion has been challenged in recent years, schools continue to play an important role in socializing children and in providing them with the knowledge and skills they will need as adults in our society. Teachers are still viewed as having the knowledge and training necessary to teach the children appropriately. While the content and the process by which they do this are sometimes challenged by parents and others in the community, generally teachers have the power and authority to carry out their teaching function. Teachers, then, have a clearly defined role in the educational process and the prerequisite power and authority to meet their responsibilities. But what about parents—what role do they play in the education of their children?

The rift between home and school that often continues to exist today in this country is partly the result of a commonly held belief that the education of the child is best left to the "educators." This belief is a natural outgrowth of the role schools have played in the past—socializing the child into a common culture. Today, many parents believe that teachers know their child better than they do. Parents assume that because teachers have taken courses in developmental and educational psychology they know the best way to help children learn. Parents are "just parents"; therefore, they support a teacher unquestioningly—unless something fairly drastic occurs.

Parental Involvement Discouraged

Teachers do receive extensive training in child growth and development, and they are exposed to a variety of methods to help children acquire knowledge. They have been taught that they are responsible for children's learning during the school year. However, formal teacher training generally provides the teacher with little information about working with parents. In fact, the lack of parental involvement in many schools is a two-sided coin, in that the schools as well as the parents minimize the importance of parental impact and often actively discourage all but the most cursory involvement. Even if teachers begin their careers with high ideals about involving parents, they are too often socialized to the view that parents don't belong in school. As a result they learn both subtle and blunt ways of shutting parents out. Other teachers may be open to encouraging parents to be more involved in the education of their children, but too often they receive little or no support for this either from the school or from their peers. Instead, they learn to close the classroom door—shutting parents out.

Parents' Roles Usurped

In addition to the influence of history on parental involvement and the present-day avoidance of parental involvement in the classroom, another sort of struggle may also account for the rift between home and school. As children begin school, they are making a separation from their parents; it is an important step on their way to independence.

Prior to schooling, parents are the children's primary caregivers—providing everything from physical care to learning experiences to emotional support. As children enter school, however, another significant person enters their lives—the teacher. Even the word is enough to bring forth an image of what parents both want for their child and fear to some degree: a warm, accepting human being who receives the child with open arms, ready to provide a challenging early school experience. If the parents prepare the child for school in a positive way, the child is anxious to please and quick to respond to the new experience and the new adult. In the process, it is very easy for parents to feel displaced. They have prepared their child to enjoy school, and they do. Not only do they enjoy school, they use the teacher as a reference point: "Ms. Kalinowski never does that." Now, how do the parents respond? How do they maintain their role in their children's lives in the face of this new, and threatening, outside influence?

While parents want the best experience possible for their children, they still need to feel important to them. If they do not feel good about themselves and their own parenting, it will be very difficult for them to feel good about someone else doing well with their child. And if they are feeling good about themselves and their own parenting, they will feel their place "usurped" by a teacher who does not include them in the educational experiences of their children.

Confidence of Teachers Threatened

What about the teachers? What is happening to them while the parents are struggling with their separation anxiety? Teachers are excited by the challenge that each new group of children brings. They are ready to take on any situation and give it their best, anxious to please both the parent and the child. If they seem to be successful with the child, all is well. But if problems begin to develop, they begin to question their own ability to cope with the situation. Frequently, they don't want to raise issues with parents because they feel the parents will blame them—either subtly or openly—accusing them of not doing their jobs properly. Teachers are also reluctant to approach parents with delicate or negative information for fear that the parent will view the information as criticism and will become defensive and hostile. So they take a "wait-and-see" attitude, hoping the problem will vanish. If it doesn't, however, they are forced at some point to talk with the parent. No matter how they choose to approach the parent—with "hard facts" or in a sympathetic vein—teachers feel vulnerable in the situation, "Is the parent going to blame me for what is going on? Perhaps I have failed with this child. Now what do I do?" The teacher feels vulnerable to the parent's criticism, even if she thinks the parent is not doing a very good job either.

Both Teacher and Parent Threatened

Thus, when the teacher and parent finally come together, often each feels incompetent and hopes not to be revealed as such to the other person. Although the teacher-parent discussions focus on what is happening to the child, since neither participant is able to be open and honest because of feelings of inadequacy, the interaction is often guarded, defensive, and frustrating. "Solutions" reached under such conditions are usually temporary at best. The real power of such a coming together—a true partnership approach—is thus denied.

What does this scenario tell us? Parents "give" their child over to the teacher—believing that this is the best way for the child to receive a good education. Teachers, on the other hand, take on the task of educating the child alone, hoping that they can have a worthwhile impact on the child's life. A clear separation takes place between home and school.

Parental Involvement Crucial

According to what is being learned about parent-child interaction and children's school achievement, the situation should change. During the last fifteen years a number of research studies on preschool education and the impact of parent-child interaction have been undertaken. The results are in, and they clearly suggest that *parental involvement in the education of the child is important in terms of the child's school achievement and later success in life.*

In summarizing a number of longitudinal preschool studies, Lazar and Darlington (Consortium for Longitudinal Studies 1981) noted that factors directly related to parental involvement (such as home visits by the teacher that focus on both the parent and the child, and the development of specific program goals designed to involve parents in the educational process) were strongly related to a program's effectiveness, as measured by children's achievement during a certain time period.

Other studies of parent-child interaction and its impact on children's achievement have documented several important findings. One concerns the parent-child communication style. The use of language by the parent and the way the parent helps the child on a problem-solving task—particularly the parent's style of expanding upon what the child says and asking questions that encourage the child to think and speak—have both been found to be related to children's school achievement (Hess and Shipman 1965, Goodson and Hess 1975, Epstein and Weikart 1979).

Another finding consistently relates children's achievement to parental attitudes—both toward themselves and toward their child's education. The basic idea that seems to emerge from many of these studies is that the more the parents feel in control of their lives, the more likely their child is to do well (Douglas 1964, 1968; Hess 1980). In terms of parental attitudes about education, again the theme seems to be that the more interested and involved the parent is in the child's education, the better the child does (Radin 1972). For example, children do better when parents take the initiative in finding out what the child is doing in school, when they (parents) are able to relate easily to teachers, when they show an interest in what the child brings home from school, when they provide activities at home to extend the child's school experience, and when they present the school experience in a positive light to the child. In general, the more involved parents are, the more they want to continue and expand this involvement (Tizard 1977, 1978; Smith 1980).

Thus, research argues strongly that parents should be involved in the educational process. Bronfenbrenner says that "the involvement of the parents as partners in the enterprise provides an on-going system which can reinforce the effects of the program while it is in operation, and help to sustain them after the program ends" (as quoted in Smith 1980, p. 31).

Parents' Feelings of Inadequacy

Such is the support for bridging the gap between home and school, between parents and teachers. But the support comes from those who stand outside the educational mainstream—psychologists, administrators, sociologists, program planners, futurologists. Many parents and teachers remain to be convinced; they are ambivalent at best, and reasons exist for this ambivalence. Parents are struggling to define who they are in a society that is examining and questioning their traditional roles and functions (whether real or idealized). Parents today are aware of how important "parenting" is, even though they aren't always sure what the term implies. To help them answer that question, materials have flooded the market to provide child development information and parenting techniques. As a result parents strive to attain "Supermom" or "Superdad" status. Parents today are also struggling to define who they are in terms of their jobs or careers and to determine the kinds of relationships they want to have with other adults. Ellen Goodman (1980, p. 6) provides an apt description of the media image of Supermom and Superdad that has become the ideal to strive toward.

Supermom wakes up her 2.6 children. They go downstairs and she gives them a Grade A nutritional breakfast, which they eat, and they all go off to school without once forgetting their lunch money. Mom goes upstairs and gets dressed in her $300 Anne Klein suit and goes off to her $25,000 job, which is both creative and socially useful. After work she comes home and spends a wonderful hour *relating with the children, because, after all, the quantity of time is not important; the quality is. She then prepares a gourmet dinner for her husband. They spend time working on their meaningful relationship, after which they go upstairs, where [they have a satisfying sexual relationship].*

What about Superdad? The Superdad is always caring, sharing. He is able to leap tall emotional boundaries in a single step at the same time he is becoming Vice-President of General Motors. Fathers are supposed to be feeling, and achieving, and attending their children's school plays.

When parents cannot meet the media image, they feel incompetent, blaming themselves for not achieving Supermom or Superdad status. Thus, by the time of their child's first school experience, whether it be in a day-care or a half-day preschool program, the parents already feel guilty about placing the child in preschool (mom should be home with the child in the early years) or fearful that the teacher will discover that the child is not perfect (an extension of a not-perfect mom). Thus, when the mother faces the teacher she is afraid of being judged as inadequate. She is also ambivalent about turning the child over to another adult: wanting to turn over some of the responsibility, yet afraid of being replaced.

A Parent's Tendency to Be Overprotective

Another important factor affecting parents today is that people are choosing to have fewer children. When families consisted of two parents and a multitude of children, parents did not have the time or the energy to invest a great deal of themselves emotionally in any one child. Today, many couples or individuals are raising only one or two children, and they become the focus of the parents' hopes and dreams and energies. Parents want to share in what is happening to their children, and they seek to learn more about what will help their child to grow. When the child of today enters the classroom, he or she comes with closely attached parents.

The paradox for parents, then, is that they have available to them a wealth of information about child development, and they want to be qualitatively involved in their child's life; however, they are under greater stress themselves economically and socially, and they need support. The sense of relief that once came from turning over the education of the child to the school now makes the parent feel even more out of control.

A Teacher's Limited Influence

Teachers have parallel struggles. They, too, want to do the best possible job of educating young children. They want to be able to provide a quality program that will help each child grow and develop cognitively, socially, emotionally, and physically—a tall order. However, no matter how well designed their program is or how confident they feel about their ability to work with young children, teachers come to realize they have only a limited impact on the child because they are a part of the child's world for only a small proportion of the child's life.

When teachers work with children who respond to their techniques and the activities they provide, they want to share these successful experiences with parents. Both parents and teachers can feel good about this type of positive exchange. However, when teachers encounter problems with children, they question their own abilities and sometimes place the blame on parents: "If they were only better parents, the child would do better in school." The situation is well described by a parent who has experienced both types of interaction with teachers:

> When my oldest son was in kindergarten, I was excited and pleased to go to a parent-teacher conference. The teacher told me, 'Your son is a delightful child! I have been looking forward to meeting you.'
> However, when my youngest daughter was six and in kindergarten, I was nervous and tense before the conference. Indeed, I was told: 'Your child is so disruptive that we wonder if she should be allowed to stay in the class.' I felt angry and defensive. They thought I was an incompetent parent! How could both of these incidents happen to me? Did I really switch from being a model parent to being a poor one?

Meanings of Parental Involvement

Thus, it is easy to see why the gaps between home and school exist and why they are likely to continue, even if society, the research community, and school administrators attempt to mandate increased parental involvement. In addition, by stepping back and looking at current attempts at parental involvement we can begin to see that they frequently miss the mark because they do not address the underlying concerns of *teachers* or *parents,* nor is there a common understanding of what is meant by the term *parental involvement.*

Parental involvement has come to mean many things to many people. Unfortunately, those who use the term frequently assume that their audience defines the term as they do. In fact, when the activities identified with parental involvement are listed, the concept can legitimately encompass a wide range of approaches. According to the Random House College Dictionary (1969) "to involve" can mean "to cause to be troublesomely associated or concerned, as in something embarrassing or unfavorable; to implicate as in guilt or crime . . . to include as a necessary circumstance, condition or consequence . . . to combine inextricably . . . to affect: have a particular effect on . . . to preoccupy or absorb fully . . . to engage the interests or emotions or commitment of." Thus, the definition of *to involve* allows for a wide range of activities and different levels within each. To illustrate, in the following sections we use the different definitions of involvement as a way of categorizing different levels of parental-involvement activities. These activities suggest a range of possibilities, some of which meet the needs of some teachers and some parents, and (not incidentally) some administrators. However, we do not feel that the first five definitions, as described here, draw on the major strengths of either the parent or the teacher; they are incomplete in contrast to the kind of parental involvement we advocate, which calls for "engaging the interests, emotions and commitment" of parents and teachers.

1. to cause to be troublesomely associated or concerned, as in something embarrassing or unfavorable: to implicate as in guilt or crime.

This is clearly at the bottom of parental involvement: the oft-feared phone call or note asking the parent to contact the teacher as soon as possible. Because of the separation between home and school, the parent assumes that the child is misbehaving or not performing well. This type of parental involvement does nothing but raise the parent's anxiety. The tendency is for parents to become defensive and to anticipate the worst possible exchange. It is easy to understand why parents who have experienced this type of interaction generally take the attitude that "no news is good news," and they avoid contact with the teacher, even though, at some level, they really want to know how their child is doing.

2. to include as a necessary circumstance, condition, or consequence.

This definition implies that parents need to be included in the educational process simply because they exist. Unfortunately, this is the attitude of many teachers as they approach working with parents. "Mandatory" activities are included in this category—for example, providing parents with information about the program and the child through printed material that is sent home about the school schedule, school lunch menus, and emergency procedures. For the teacher, information-sharing at this level takes the form of report cards and the twice-yearly parent/teacher conferences. Parent meetings are another less frequently used vehicle for providing required information to parents. Programs offer parent meetings as frequently as once a week or as infrequently as once a year. The once-a-year meetings provide information to the parents about the school and occur either early in the year to orient parents to the school or later in the year to provide parents with information on what has been accomplished.

Another "necessary circumstance, condition, or consequence" for some programs (especially at the preschool level) is to include parents in the program as volunteers—an official mandate to involve parents. Head Start is a good example of a preschool program in which parents are expected to volunteer time to support the activities of the program. The hope is, of course, that by being involved in the program, parents will become more involved in the education of their child. Activities within the volunteer support category include such things as conducting public-relations activities for the program, organizing and carrying out fund-raising activities, serving on program-related committees, and volunteering to work in the classroom. But parents are often assigned menial tasks, such as helping the teacher set up the activities for the day, taking attendance, checking the children's health as they come to school, sweeping up at the end of the day, and putting away materials. While the parents are physically present in these cases, the tasks being performed seldom engage them in the educational process. This low level of involvement reinforces for parents the idea that they know nothing that would be of use to teachers. In fact, many of the tasks they are asked to do in the classroom could well be done by children, and probably should be. Thus, when parent involvement is mandated, teachers often carry it out to the letter, but the "spirit" is missing.

3. to combine inextricably.

In two ways teachers can involve parents inextricably in their child's education. One way is for teachers to show parents how they, too, are teachers as well as parents—that they are involved in the child's education already and should continue in that role. The second way is to get them involved in the structure and function of the school as decision makers.

The concept of parents as teachers has become popular as a result of recent publications in the field of psychology, sociology, and education that emphasize parents as the first and most important teachers of their own children. This concept is true, in many ways; yet to accept it is to define an additional role for parents. At a time when people are struggling with the concept of *parenting*, they are also being asked to think of themselves as *teachers*. Ellen Goodman (1980) summarizes the dilemma very well:

> We are feeling guilty not only because we don't fulfill the old roles, but because we don't fulfill the new roles either. Our inadequacy is brought home to us by those wonderful people, the early childhood people. Now we are told that if we don't hang the right mobile over the crib at 18 months, our children will never get into Harvard at 18 years. . . . I'm grateful my daughter was four before I found out it was all over at three. This has helped our relationship enormously (p. 6).

Her open and honest statement expresses the feeling of many parents today. But the popular trend is still to recognize the role of parent as teacher and to formalize it in relation to the child's school experience. Teachers who adopt this concept prepare materials for parents to use at home with the child—materials that are related to activities occurring in the classroom. Teachers can show parents how to use the materials with their children at home so that the school learning experiences will be reinforced and extended. The actual activity, the materials to be used, the approach to "teaching" the child, and the appropriate amount of time that should be spent on the task are all determined by the teacher.

While the teacher in this situation may feel that she is able to have an impact on the child's home life, the parents frequently feel overwhelmed and powerless. Many parents either don't want to be or can't be teachers of their children in the most formal sense.

The other way to "combine parents inextricably" is to involve them in the decision-making process of the structure and content of a school's program. In the Head Start preschool program, for example, parents must be included in the decision-making process. They are involved in hiring personnel and defining program priorities, as mandated by national guidelines. Other programs with similar requirements for parental involvement create parent advisory councils or boards that have no decision-making power but that are designed to provide a mechanism for potential input into the program. The assumption is that involving parents as policy makers establishes an arena in which parents can express their goals for the program and help to determine program direction.

4. to affect: have a particular effect on.

One category of parent involvement—parent education—falls outside the day-to-day operations of the school program and the direct relationship between teacher, parent, and child. However, it is a widespread phenomenon in our society, implying ways for parents to be involved in their child's education. Parent education programs, books, and materials have been designed to meet the needs of parents all through the parenting years—prenatally through adult life.

Infant programs are designed to provide parents with information and parenting skills that help them develop self-confidence in their new role, as in the High/Scope Parent-to-Parent Model (Evans and Halpern, 1981). Programs designed for parents of preschoolers frequently deal with issues related to behavior management (Systematic Training for Effective Parenting—STEP). Other parent education materials have been developed for parents of school-age children and adolescents (Parent Effectiveness Training—PET) that provide parents information about what the child is going through at these developmental stages and ways in which parents can learn to handle a variety of situations.

Many parent-education activities are helpful to parents; they provide information about and an understanding of a child at specific stages of development as well as some techniques that parents can use to handle everyday situations. This type of support is extremely important when families feel isolated and do not have available the more traditional supports and the wisdom of the extended family.

Some parent-education programs attempt to integrate ethnic parental goals. Others, however, reflect only middle-class white American perspectives, failing to take into account the range of current family styles and the ethnic diversity in the United States.

5. *to preoccupy or absorb fully.*

Parent cooperative school programs are examples of preoccupied parental involvement. In these programs, parents collectively assume full responsibility for the children's educational program. They are "fully absorbed" because they are responsible for program design, day-to-day management issues, the classroom curriculum and how it is carried out, fiscal management, physical location, program maintenance, and monitoring.

Parents who can maintain this level of involvement are not those who must work fulltime. Teachers in cooperative schools interact with parents constantly. Available time for the teacher to be involved with the parent in areas relating to a child's growth and development is important. What is assured is that the parents have an integral role in defining the goals of the program and making decisions affecting the ways in which the program is implemented. They know what is going on and why, and they have the power to make changes if everyone agrees that it would be in the best interests of all concerned.

6. *to engage the interests or emotions or commitment of.*

This level of parental involvement is seldom attained; but it has the greatest benefits for parents, teachers, and children. Teachers must take the initiative if this level of parental involvement is to be achieved. First, they have to believe that the parent has something to offer. Then they must invite the parent to enter into a partnership in which parent and teacher work together in the service of the child. They must be able to make parents feel competent about their parenting—not for the information they *can* receive, or the teaching they can *learn* to do, or the parenting skills they *can* develop—but for what they already know about their child: those things that hurt the child's feelings, that the child is able to put on a jacket, the things that motivate the child or that inhibit the child, how the child likes to use the left hand for drawing and the right for eating, and how the child acts with siblings and others in the family. This information provides the context for expanding the teacher's knowledge of the child; it outlines the framework within which the child operates outside of the classroom. When parents see that the information they provide is truly helpful to teachers (and they will see this if the teachers show parents how they use the information to help plan activities with a particular child), they will be more capable of learning about what the teacher has observed and knows about their child. A sense of trust develops between the two parties: both the parent and the teacher are concerned about the child's growth and development. As parents provide their observations, the teacher, in turn, provides parents with child-development information that puts the parents' observations into perspective. For example, if a parent is feeling that the child is very selfish, never wanting to share anything, the teacher can respond by telling the parent, "This is a stage that all children go through. It takes children time to understand the idea of sharing."

Other ways exist for achieving this level of parental involvement. For example, instead of simply sending notes home to inform parents of school procedures, teachers can send something home weekly that the child has done in school, or they can provide a brief description of something the child did during the week to let the parent know on a regular basis what is happening.

Parent meetings can also "engage the interests or emotions or commitment" of parents. For example, some school programs plan a series of parent meetings with guest speakers and specific topics to be covered for the entire year. At the first meeting a full-year schedule is given to the parents so that they can choose to come to meetings that are of interest to them. Another technique is to gather the parents together early in the school year and work with them to define what they want to do in the parent meetings, using the resources of the program if they so desire, but drawing on other community resources if that is more appropriate. Obviously, the latter approach provides for greater parental involvement in the process, greater parental control over the direction of the meetings, and (not incidentally) greater parental participation in parent meetings during the school year. When parents are involved in making choices, they have a much greater investment in attending the meetings.

Another instance calling for the interests, emotions, and commitment of parents and teachers occurs when a child experiences school problems and parents and teachers realize they must resolve them together; for, without the other's cooperation, individual solutions will fail. For example, a preschool child may often use crying as a way of seeking attention in the classroom. One teacher adopted a strategy whereby every time the child cried as a means of getting attention, she offered him a choice. He could stop crying and remain with the group or sit in the "green chair" (a "time-out" chair separated from, but in view of, the class) until he was ready to join the others. The child made his own choice and eventually chose to stay with the rest of the class, finding that his manipulative use of tears did not get him the attention he wanted. In a conference with the child's parents a few weeks later, the teacher discovered that they were having a terrible time at home with the child's crying. The teacher listened to their grievance, then shared her way of handling the situation, suggesting to the parents that perhaps the child's crying was worse at home because he could no longer get his way by crying at school. The parents decided to use a technique similar to what the teacher had developed and several weeks later reported that things had improved at home.

This type of information sharing between home and school allows for teacher-parent communication about common problems and for the development of workable solutions. When such communication is lacking, either the parent or the teacher can unwittingly sabotage the efforts of the other; but when such communication exists, parents and teachers can come together in a spirit of cooperation, viewing the child as an entity apart from themselves who can benefit from their combined efforts—from their "partnership."

Through this process of partnership and sharing, parents and teachers begin to realize their goals for the child, recognizing common goals and allowing for differences of opinion. Rather than viewing each other with distrust and misgiving, the parent and the teacher begin to understand each other's point of view and discover to what extent they can work together and where they need to "let go" of some goals because they would be working at cross purposes.

This new level of parental involvement seems perfect: parents and teachers coming together to plan the best possible experiences for the child, respecting each other's views, allowing for individual differences, planning together how to accomplish mutually defined goals. The reality is that neither the teacher nor the parent can maintain this level of involvement for a long period of time. We have defined our "ideal," just as we defined "Supermom" and "Superdad" earlier. We have in fact just described "Superteacher"! To fall short of the level of involvement described here should not create guilt in teachers. That is not the intent of this article. What we hope to accomplish is to make teachers and parents aware of what each of them can contribute to a child's school experience, to begin to recognize that they can learn from each other, and to think about ways they can support each other (if only minimally) rather than viewing each other as adversaries.

In a society where people are feeling more and more isolated, Bronfenbrenner's words ring true: "The strategy of choice becomes that of building interconnections between the settings in which people live out their lives, so that family roles receive recognition and validation outside the home in the contexts of preschool, school, neighborhood and work" (1979, p. 103).

References

Bronfenbrenner, U. 1974. Is early intervention effective? *A report on longitudinal programs*, vol. 2. DHEW Publication Number OHD, 74-24.

_____. 1979a. Beyond the deficit model in child and family policy. *Teachers College Record* 81: 95–104.

_____. 1979b. *The ecology of human development: experiments by nature and design.* Cambridge: Harvard University Press.

_____. 1980. On making human beings human. *Character* 2.

Central Advisory Council for Education (England).

Consortium for Longitudinal Studies. 1981. *Lasting effects of early education.* Monographs of the Society for Research in Child Development.

Douglas, J. W. B., Ross, J. M., and Simpson, H. R. 1968. *All our future.* London: Peter Davies.

Douglas, J. W. B. 1964. *The home and the school.* London: McGibbon and Kee.

Epstein, A. S., and Weikart, D. P. 1979. *The Ypsilanti-Carnegie Infant Education Project.* Monographs of the High/Scope Educational Research Foundation, no. 6.

Evans, J. E., and Halpern, R. 1981. *Dissemination of the High/Scope Parent-to-Parent Model: lessons learned.* Ypsilanti, MI: High/Scope Foundation.

Fantini, M. and Cardenas, R., eds. 1980. *Parenting in a multicultural society.* New York: Longman.

Getzels, J. W. 1974. Socialization and education: a note on discontinuities. In *The family as educator,* ed., H. Leichter. New York: Teachers College Press.

Goodman, E. 1980. Observations on parenting and the women's movement. In *Parenting in a changing society.* ERIC/EECE. Urbana: University of Illinois.

Goodson, B. D. and Hess, R. D. 1975. *Parents as teachers of young children: an evaluative review of some contemporary concepts and programs.* Stanford, CA: Stanford University Press.

Hess, R. D. 1980. Experts and amateurs: some unintended consequences of parent education. In *Parenting in a multicultural society,* eds. M. Fantini and R. Cardenas. New York: Longman.

Hess, R. D. and Shipman, V. C. 1965. Early experience and the socialization of cognitive modes in children. *Child Development* 36.

Lightfoot, S. L. 1978. *Worlds apart: relationships between families and schools.* New York: Basic Books.

Little, A. and Smith, G. 1971. *Strategies of compensation: a review of educational projects for the disadvantaged in the United States.* Paris: Centre for Educational Research and Innovation, Organization for Economic Cooperation and Development.

Markel, G. and Greenbaum, J. 1981. Assertiveness training for parents of disabled children. *Exceptional Parent.*

Plowden Report. 1967. *Children and their primary schools.* London: HMSO.

Powell, D. R. 1980. Toward a socio-ecological perspective of relations between parents and child care programs. In *Advances in early education and day care* vol. 1, ed. S. Kilmer. New York: JAI Press.

Radin, N. 1972. Three degrees of maternal involvement in a preschool program: impact on mothers and children. *Child development* 43.

Schweinhart, L. J. and Weikart, D. P. 1980. *Young children grow up: the effects of the Perry Preschool Program on youths through age 15.* Monographs of the High/Scope Educational Research Foundation, no. 7. Ypsilanti, MI: High/Scope Press.

Smith, T. 1980. *Parents and preschool.* Oxford Preschool Research Project, vol. 6. Ypsilanti, MI: High/Scope Press.

Tizard, B. 1978. Carry on communicating. *Times Educational Supplement.*

———. 1977. No common ground. *Times Educational Supplement.*

Weber, C. U., Foster, P. W. and Weikart, D. P. 1978. *An economic analysis of the Ypsilanti Perry Preschool Project.* Monographs of the High/Scope Educational Research Foundation, no. 4. Ypsilanti, MI: High/Scope Press.

Zigler, E., Cascione, R. 1980. On being a parent. In *Parenthood in a changing society* ERIC/EECE. Urbana: University of Illinois.

Strategies for a Successful Parental Involvement Program

*Professor of child development and family life at Western Illinois
University, Dr. Mona S. Johnston has also held other positions that
recommend her as a contributor to this book of readings. She has directed
a child-development laboratory and has coordinated a university
preschool and infant center. Dr. Johnston received the Outstanding
Educator of America Award in 1972.*

> *To be effective coordinators of the people and forces that are
> shaping their children, parents must have voice so they do not have
> to rely on people or programs they do not respect. Parents who are
> secure, supported, valued, and in control of their lives are more ef-
> fective parents (Kenniston 1977, p. 2).*

Why is parental involvement important? What makes effective parental involvement so difficult? What can be done to revitalize parental
involvement? These are critical questions worthy of thought by educators, administrators, and parents.

Parents and early childhood educators exert vital influences on young
children's development even though they function in different social
contexts. In order to best serve young children responsibly, parents and
teachers must build a partnership on the bedrock of mutual respect, understanding of each other's perspective, and awareness of the far-
reaching influence that partnership is likely to exert on the well-being
of everyone involved.

The Status of Parental Involvement

Parental involvement carries significant but varied meanings for the professionals serving young children. For some, the term means excitement, teamwork, new ideas, and fellowship; for others, it means mandates from the administrators, unreasonableness, indifference, apathy from parents, and feelings of pressure to comply with one more guideline and do one more job. Although an occasional experience may be at one of these extremes or the other, most professionals' past experiences tend to fall somewhere in the middle of the continuum. Since that is true, what are some general principles and guidelines that can be applied to a variety of early childhood programs in order to have viable parental involvements?

Parental involvement is not a new concept. Historically, parents have always cared for, taught, trained, and disciplined children as a part of the children's socialization process. Ideas of philosophers and educators influenced thinking about early childhood education and parental involvement as early as the 18th and 19th centuries. Rousseau, Pestalozzi and Froebel recognized and promoted the role parents have in child development, and contemporary education bears the marks of their influence.

At the turn of the century professional organizations such as PTA and Child Study Association came into existence, serving as stepping stones to formal parental involvement in early childhood education. In 1909, the federal government held the first White House Conference on Care of Dependent Children, which led to the establishment of the Children's Bureau publication *Infant Care.*

During the 1960s and 1970s, the nation focused on early childhood education and parental involvement, primarily because of the Russians' launching of Sputnick and the impressive body of research on the significance early experiences have on the future development of young children. Research also pointed out, with overwhelming evidence, that parental involvement and family background were positively correlated with children's academic achievement.

In response to these developments, the federal government launched its programs War On Poverty and the Great Society, committing abundant resources for continuing research and programming nationwide. With this research in mind, the guidelines for many early childhood programs such as Head Start, Home Start, Right to Read, Elementary and Secondary Act, and the Education of the Handicapped Act mandate parental involvement in policy making and program implementation.

The dilemma of parents in contemporary society is that they feel alone in their responsibility for child-rearing and their children's conduct, yet inadequate to teach the child satisfactorily. "American parents today are worried and uncertain about how to bring up their children. . . . [They] wonder whether they are doing a good job as parents, yet are unable to define just what a good job is. In droves, they seek expert advice" (Kenniston 1977, p. 3). Like parents, most early childhood educators are also concerned about the well-being of the children. Yet, early childhood educators who are concerned and parents who care often cannot come together in their strategies to serve the children. Each feels alone and somewhat guilty.

Our challenge lies in finding creative strategies that translate these mandates and research findings into the dynamic involvement of teachers and parents.

As educators, sometimes we tend to shift the responsibility for ineffective parental involvement onto the parents. We observe their apparent lack of interest and concern based on their poor attendance and lack of enthusiasm for school-sponsored parental involvement activities. They appear defensive during the parent-teacher conferences designed for periodical review of the children's progress. But are we doing anything to invite parental involvement and to understand the parents' viewpoint on the children's education? Since the responsibility for ineffective parent-teacher involvement rests on both parents and teachers, as teachers we need to consciously examine and reassess our perceptions, using a perspective that encompasses parents and their daily lifestyles as well as our commitment to teaching young children.

Teachers and children usually form a primary dyad, leaving parents as peripheral and marginal members of the group. Most parents are deeply involved with their children and concerned with all the forces that affect the children; in this dyad situation they perceive themselves as less than full members of the group and may react defensively or apathetically toward overtures by the educators. In turn, early childhood educators respond to parental nonresponsive or defensive behavior with disdain, and find warm, open, candid, and objective communication with parents burdensome. Therefore, educators tend to limit their involvement with parents to a minimum, sometimes fulfilling mandated requirements by scheduling periodic social or formal meetings with a fixed agenda they have prepared for the parents.

One version of these meetings may be periodic parent-teacher conferences scheduled at fifteen minute intervals for a couple of days, usually twice a year. During the allocated fifteen minutes, five minutes are spent talking about the weather or other chitchat. The next five to seven minutes are dedicated to going over the sheet that the teacher has filled out evaluating the child. Another minute or so is devoted to reviewing any written comments. This leaves about three minutes for parents to discuss their child with the teacher and share their own experiences and observations. In the meantime, the teacher is glancing at her watch, and the parents scheduled for the next appointment are peeking into the room. The parents may still be assimilating the content of the evaluation form and may feel frustrated because of the limited dialogue and unanswered questions. If the parents experienced a similar situation last semester and believe they will probably experience it again and again in the future, this frustration may be further compounded. They are likely to feel helpless, frustrated, and inferior for not having any control over the situation. Many of us who teach young children are also parents who have had similar experiences in the past, and we should be able to empathize with "our" parents when they face the same frustration.

The early childhood educators' feelings are likely to be similar to those of the parents—anesthesia accompanied with a sense of temporary relief that the ordeal is over for another few months. They may also feel a residue of frustration, anger, helplessness, loss of personal worth, and a gnawing sense of failure to nurture and develop parental involvement.

These experiences reinforce the indifference between parents and teachers. Since humans seek to avoid discomfort and painful experiences, some parents may toss the announcement of the next parent-teacher activity into the wastepaper basket. There may be some parents who come to the event because of their commitment to their children, but who communicate their apathy through lack of enthusiasm for these school-sponsored parental involvement programs. Thus, teachers and parents slip further apart. Early childhood educators feel defeated because their efforts to involve parents do not produce the desired outcomes, and parents feel like second-class citizens whose opinions and feelings receive little attention from the teachers. This exaggerates the parent-child versus teacher-child dyads, creates increasing distance between parents and teachers, and causes enormous tension for young children caught between the parents and the teachers, who are each feeling alone, helpless and ineffective in their respective responsibilities.

It is not, then, that parents are irresponsible, selfish, and apathetic in their responsibility toward their children. They simply feel vulnerable in their roles because they lack authority over some organizations and agencies that take an active part in child rearing. In fact,

> most parents deal with those others from a position of inferiority or helplessness. As a result, the parent today is usually a coordinator without voice or authority, a maestro trying to conduct an orchestra of players who have never met and who play from a multitude of different scores, each in a notation the conductor cannot read. If parents are frustrated, it is no wonder, for although they have the responsibility for their children's lives, they hardly ever have the voice, the authority, or the power to make others listen to them (Kenniston 1977, p. 18).

Thus, while parents are responsible for the well-being of their children, a series of diverse forces contribute to child rearing. Yet most of these social institutions have relegated the parents to the back of the stage while still holding them accountable. Ideally, the relationship between the parents and service agencies should be reversed: Parents should decide which services to consume and when, and should have a say in their children's early education. And parents and teachers should develop a meaningful and binding "teamwork" relationship.

Importance of Teacher-Parent Partnership

The common area of parents' and teachers' responsibility is children. For the parents a child is their biological and emotional offspring; they have vested interests in providing the very best they can with the material and human resources available to them. Early childhood educators have a professional commitment to the young children in their care by virtue of their chosen profession, and the years of preparation that trained them to serve children in nursery schools, day care centers, Head Start, and other early childhood programs. Since parents and teachers both have strong allegiance to children, they can best serve them by developing mutually supportive relationships.

Early childhood educators need to recognize, encourage, and enhance the primary attachment between parents and children. It is this relationship that helps children develop basic trust, personal identity, autonomy, and positive self-concepts. During the process of giving routine care, parents communicate their love to their children, providing a warm, consistent, and responsive atmosphere. The children learn that they are lovable and important human beings. These messages, verbal and nonverbal, that they register form the core of positive self-concepts and encourage them to explore, manipulate, inquire, and experiment within the home base. Their exploratory behaviors pave the way for them to discover their bodies, learn about the properties of objects, and the relationships among objects, events, and persons. Therefore, positive feedback from the parents sets children free to venture with confidence into secondary environments such as preschool programs, playgrounds, and other neighborhood locations. In Bloom's opinion, "It is the adults in the home who serve to stimulate the child's intellectual development, and it is the adults in the home who determine the basic preparation of the child for later learning in the school" (Bloom 1981, p. 77).

As children enter preschool programs, they bring with them the previous experiences, attitudes, and self-concepts that the early childhood educators will have to work with. Home continues to be the secure base that encourages children to reach out, touch, explore, and experiment to expand their physical, social, and cognitive worlds. Therefore, the primary relationships pave the way to developing warm, secure secondary relationships; and these interactions with teachers, doctors, cooks, and aides can continue to feed the self-esteem of children. When parents and teachers understand, respect, and work with each other, the transition from home to school becomes easier for children. In fact, to a degree, home and school can become extensions of each other, thus fulfilling the objectives of both the parents and the early childhood educators.

The quality of parent-child relationships also determines how well the children will progress in their other development at school. Warm, supportive relationships at home help children form satisfying relationships with their peers and teachers. In turn, these relationships help the children feel the self-confidence and the sense of belonging that promotes new knowledge and skills in cognitive, social-emotional, and physical areas. These new skills again reinforce their feelings of personal worth and the positive growth continues. Thus warm, positive relationships and stimulating environments at home facilitate the acquisition of new skills at school. Expanding the security base between home and school helps children understand the relationship between past skills and new acquisitions, particularly in their social development.

While it is important that parents and teachers work together to maximize the impact of preschool education on young children, this is possible only if the "parents [are] sufficiently involved in the nursery school to understand its importance for their child and to give support and reinforcement to the learning objectives and tasks of [early childhood education]" (Bloom 1981, p. 83). With the impressive body of knowledge substantiating the impact of early education in the development of young children (Gordon 1975; Honig and Lally 1981; White 1975), we know that the influence of early education can be far-reaching if there is mutual support and involvement between parents and early childhood educators.

Strategies for Mutual Support

Prerequisites to a dynamic partnership between parents and teachers include understanding each other's responsibilities, commitment to building each other's self-esteem and sense of competence, and dedication to and support of each other's efforts in meeting the responsibilities unique to particular roles.

Skills

Both parents and teachers have unique skills to bring to the parent-teacher partnership. As children enter preschool programs, parents continue to provide emotional support and to meet children's various needs. The family allows children to vent their concerns, doubts, fears, and uncertainties without recrimination; it also celebrates their successes and new achievements at school that can enhance and facilitate the objectives of early childhood programs. Parents help teach their children the routines of work, play, rest, and study. Skills learned at school are positively reinforced and supported by the parents, furthering the children's learning. For example, listening skills taught at school can be encouraged at home as bedtime stories are read to children accompanied by questions that ask the children to tell them the story or expand on it. Number concepts learned at school can be practiced when the parents take children marketing by counting oranges, the number of steps between the parking lot and the store, and so on. Observation skills may be put to use when parents quiz children to spot different objects or events during the routines of daily living. Parents also contribute toward children's development when they provide a variety of experiences such as vacations, picnics, trips to zoos, museums, parks, and other community and seasonal events. These broad experiences sharpen children's observational skills, increase their general awareness about the world and the events around them while encouraging their curiosity. Educators can then build upon these experiences through specific learning activities. Parents also facilitate the objectives of early childhood programs as they share their aspirations and standards of performance with their children. By doing so, parents serve as models and mentors, helping children acquire personal work habits as well as setting standards for their personal performance (Dave 1963, Wolf 1966, Marjoribanks 1979 as cited in Bloom 1981). In addition, early childhood educators have specific skills and knowledge that are not only helpful for children, but worthwhile resources for parents. Teachers know the principles of human development and understand patterns of development in young children. They also can design appropriate learning environments for children that harmonize with their developmental abilities, setting short- and long-range objectives for children based on each child's abilities. This information can be an asset for parents as they formulate goals for their children. White (1979) identified the one major hurdle families face that hinders them in helping their children as parental lack of knowledge regarding the process of child development. Early childhood educators can be a valuable resource in this area, helping parents set realistic goals for their children by making them aware of the specific skills and abilities of their children at a given level of development. They can also guide parents in choosing appropriate play items and activities This professional help provides parents with basic knowledge and assists them in understanding, accepting, and relating to their children in a more satisfactory manner.

Self-esteem
Parents and teachers can strengthen their partnership further by generating and affirming each other's sense of competence. It is not

uncommon for parents and teachers who live and work with children to seek affirmation that they are doing a good job. Everyone needs this feedback. Hayakawa (1963) states that "the basic purpose of all human activity is the protection, the maintenance, and the enhancement, not of self, but of the self-concept . . ." (p. 37). Self-esteem is developed within the context of social interaction. Adult responses to children develop children's self-esteem. For adults—parents and teachers—this affirmation comes from within themselves. However, this internal feedback system is developed, refined, and sustained by consistent input from other adults who are perceived as important in their social environment. Therefore, even competent parents and early childhood educators need to provide positive feedback to each other regarding their unique contributions toward children's development. The need for affirmation of competence is even greater for parents and teachers because their hours are long, and their jobs are tedious, providing limited financial rewards. Major satisfaction comes from the long-term wholesome development of children and the children's consequent self-esteem. But only those parents and early childhood educators who have self-esteem and a personal sense of competence can provide the same positive feedback to young children.

Teamwork

Time and energy are limited resources for both the parents and the teachers. Each is under pressure to meet unending deadlines. Teamwork between parents and teachers can help maximize results for both; for example, some of the parents' specific skills can help teachers in their routine responsibilities. One of the parents in our preschool program is a secretary. She has helped do the newsletter for several years, and her professional expertise provides a tremendous service to the staff; it would take them much longer to do the newsletter with less impressive results. Her effort has been deeply appreciated by the staff, and she has felt good about her contribution to her child's program. She has also received positive comments from other parents. Following suit, the other parents are more willing to help. Similarly, some of the parents saw the market order form designed to arrange the basic six food groups in columns that identify the amounts to be ordered and the prices for each item. These columns help integrate the special weekly buys at the local grocery stores. These forms were shared with the parents, who appreciated using them. In another program, an annual workshop on educational toys is presented to help the participants choose play items for young children. On this occasion, special invitations are mailed to grandparents as well. Some of the reputable dealers for children's play equipment do the displays on site. Any orders that are placed during the workshop permit the parents or grandparents to buy durable, educational toys for their children at a discount. Another successful strategy to maximize results for both home and school can be the tradition some early childhood programs have of offering parents opportunities to buy prepared food. One day a week a given food item is prepared in large quantity and made available to parents at a very reasonable cost. These items are listed in the newsletter, usually one item a week on a fixed day. Parents place their orders by Monday each week to facilitate the market order. Then on Thursday when they pick up their children, they also pick up their order. Since only the quantity of the food prepared has increased, the cook's marketing and preparation time is not affected significantly, and this can be a real help for working parents. Also, children feel they are sharing when a favorite item off their menu comes home with them. Some popular items have been meatballs, chili, brownies, chocolate chip cookies, goulash, monkey bread, twenty-four-hour salad, and lasagna.

Parents can volunteer to help clean, rearrange, and decorate the classrooms and play-yards, provided childcare and a simple snack or lunch is available on a Saturday or a vacation day. Some of the parents may take the responsibility for childcare while one of the staff volunteers to prepare the snack or lunch for the working group. Occasionally parents repair toys, paint wall murals, and hold school yard sales for preschool programs. Our parents and teachers put together a very successful activity booklet "When We Do It Together: Parents and Children" to share with other members of the community.

Teachers can come in a little early or leave a little late at the end of a given day to accommodate a parent's schedule or an urgent need to share a concern. Some parents and teachers are willing to take a late lunch hour in order to share ideas about programs, maximize results, and promote the give-and-take relationships between parents and educators. Whatever is done, each program has unique sets of talents and needs that can be tapped to help promote teamwork between parents and educators.

The challenge of humanizing and revitalizing the significant relationship between parents and teachers can be unique, exciting, and fulfilling; for it stretches our creativity, resourcefulness, and imagination. We can discover personal attributes and potentials that would otherwise lie dormant. But this challenge has to be an *integral* part of the philosophy and objectives of any childhood program. Our basic premise has to be that parent involvement is a *process*, not an event, which must include the parents in planning, implementation, and assessment of the total program.

Obstacles to Parental Involvement

Difficulties that hinder successful interaction between early childhood educators and parents are complex and varied. Major forces blocking meaningful interaction include lack of motivation, inadequate communication, limited human and material resources, and a possible lack of organizational skills. Each of these barriers requires a closer examination so that some alternatives and strategies may be considered to help rectify the situation.

Lack of Motivation

One of the major obstacles early childhood educators contend with is a lack of motivation in educators, administrators, and parents. Lack of motivation among some educators may be triggered by the poor success rate of previous attempts to involve parents. They may also have discouraging flashbacks of the amounts of energy and time these unsuccessful activities took. Some educators feel secure and comfortable only with the conventional approaches, whether these are successful or not. Therefore, they prefer the status quo of routine parent-teacher conferences and one or two social events a year to comply with the policy mandates rather than risking effort on other alternatives. Lack of motivation among administrators may be prompted by some of the same reasons as among educators, but they may also have the added reason of budgetary restrictions because of budget cuts or inflation. In this case, their major concern might simply focus on compliance with program guidelines.

Parents' apathy may stem from a variety of reasons. Like teachers, they have complex life styles and responsibilities that sap their energy and time. Their past experiences in parent involvement activities may have been negative, and they may have sensed a lack of concern for parental perspective among educators. They may also feel teachers blamed them for their children's difficulties. Poor participation, sometimes interpreted as lack of motivation, may be caused by unsuitable meeting times, the choice of activities, and obligations to fulfill other family responsibilities such as household work, marketing, or child care for younger children. Occasionally, the lack of motivation among parents may stem from the fact that teachers represent an authoritarian image.

Poor Communication

Inadequate, lopsided, and formal communication between home and school is another major obstacle in achieving effective parent-teacher relationships. This type of communication may reinforce some of the negative images parents have of authority figures, based on firsthand encounters or formed from others' experiences. Sometimes the formal structure of preschool programs can intimidate and alienate parents further through highly impersonal correspondence. Parents may feel powerless against such formality, especially when communication tends to be one-sided, coming from the school to the parents. In many instances, the only communication the parents see involves directives about fees, permission slips, bake sales, and similar items related to policies of the program. While there is nothing wrong with periodic bulletins or newsletters, if they are the sole mode of communication with parents, they may reinforce rather than dissolve the obstacles to participation.

Implicit in the process of effective communication is the concept that a dialogue is occurring between parents and early childhood educators. Pierce (1972) describes communication in daily interaction as a process of sharing understandings and attitudes, of working toward congruence, or determining how and where there are agreements and differences of opinions. This description implies a shared understanding of the language being used and assumes enough mutual respect, acceptance, concern, and empathy between communicating persons that they can explore their differences of opinions freely without loss of self-esteem and recrimination.

Since messages are communicated verbally and nonverbally, factors such as tone and quality of voice, body posture, facial expression, physical appearance, eye contact, and physical distance between speakers affect the quality of communication. A pleasant and warm voice, physical closeness, and eye contact sets up positive communication. Language that is simple, precise, and clear minus the educational jargon is also essential. If the teacher needs to point out to the parent the need for additional large muscle activity for their child, rather than stating it as a need for gross motor activity, she can mention that the child needs more play, such as climbing the jungle jim and parallel bars or riding a tricycle. Although cultivating communication places considerable challenge and responsibility on early childhood educators, most parents will respond to warm, caring, and spontaneous interaction as well as children do.

Limited Parental Contact

Parents, like teachers, experience heavy demands on their time and energy, particularly in households with two wage earners or in single-parent families headed by the mother. In our society, mothers are still expected to be the primary nurturers of their children. Even though they may work, most of them still feel very responsible for their young children and experience deep-seated guilt because they are separated from the children during working hours. While both parents should play a dynamic role in parent involvement, mothers of young children have a particularly unique need for ongoing, informal dialogue with educators in order to keep in touch with their children's world. They need to receive continual reassurance about their children's well-being. One way to help them feel a sense of continuity and participation in their children's daily lives may be to use a variety of modes to communicate with them. Different ways of relating and sharing with them will spur their interest and involvement with early childhood educators. Since most early childhood educators tend to be women, and traditionally mothers participate in parent-teacher meetings, fathers seem to be left out of parental involvement. Special efforts need to be made to involve both parents when possible.

Limited Resources and Skills

Lack of motivation and inadequate communication, when accompanied with limited or inadequate resources and poor organizational skills, will cause parental involvement to come to a halt. Inadequate resources refer to lack of human and material resources needed to accomplish a given task. When early childhood educators are overworked, they cannot devote adequate time and energy to parental involvement. Besides human resources, they also need material resources to launch various projects, such as paper, postage, typing assistance, and other items necessary to implement parental involvement activities. To optimize the use of both material and human resources, we need to have organizational and managerial skills. If these resources or skills are lacking, they may affect the quality of the relationship among parents, staff, and administrators.

Poor management and organization can contribute to lack of motivation and poor communication, and lack of material and human resources can cause other educators, parents, and administrators to pull their resources away. Thus, any one of these, or a combination of them, can be obstacles to parental development.

Strategies for Involvement

Developing effective parental involvement is not impossible. Besides working at specific problem areas, developing a good rapport with parents and setting up a viable parental involvement program takes time, concerted effort, creativity, and cooperation. Occasionally, because of our personal needs or professional demands for accomplishment, we expect consequential results in a short time. We need to remind ourselves and those around us that it takes a lot of time and effort for an assortment of persons to become a fully functioning group. We are all acquainted with the rapid pace of life and the competing demands made on both early childhood educators and parents. Thus, parents and teachers may hesitate to undertake additional commitments. However, as they expend time and energy to reach common goals, they will recognize the significance of teamwork, experience satisfaction from successful interaction, and renew their pledge to continued teamwork. Since each parent is different, not all parents are likely to respond in the same manner at the same time to our efforts to involve them. It will be relatively easy to involve some parents and not others, partially because of personality characteristics, past experiences with other educators and school administrators, and existing constraints of personal and professional lives. Therefore, while reaching out to hard-to-reach parents, we must combine patience with a variety of involvement methods, such as working with the children, admission forms, parent groups, informal contacts, newsletters, and shared school time.

Work with Children

Some of the most important initial involvement gets communicated to the parents through their children. If parents see that their children are happy and fond of their preschool program, the parents already have a positive mind set toward open communication with the school. Moreover, children are the best publicity agents for programs. Their faces, actions, and enthusiasm more than compensate for their slight lack of sophisticated verbal skills to express their enjoyment.

If early childhood educators tend to "be off-handed, be cold toward the child . . . parents can never work closely with you. . . . To touch the child is to touch the parent. To praise the child is to praise the parent. To criticize the child is to hit the parent. The two are two, but the two are one." (Hymes 1974, p. 9). Therefore, positive relationships between early childhood educators and children is a very good beginning in reaching and relating to parents.

The Admission Form

Teachers can gather some basic information to help involvement at the time of the child's admission to the program by using the admission form as a data collection instrument. Teachers will want to know the current or previous career or occupation of both parents; their academic backgrounds; individual hobbies and crafts; their membership in organizations; vacations that families have enjoyed the most; special family rituals such as birthdays, holidays, or special family days, including which activities parents enjoy and which ones the children enjoy. This information can be organized and transcribed on five-by-seven-inch cards to develop a valuable resource file on parents' hobbies, interests, and skills. It is also useful to know which of the children's parents are close friends, for they should work well together.

At the beginning of the school year, a roster of the children with their parent's names, addresses, phone numbers, and the children's dates of birth should be developed and given to all parents, other teachers, and administrators. Several support systems can be initiated from these rosters, such as car-pools, babysitting arrangements, play groups for children during weekends and vacations, and social interaction at home and school. Data such as children's allergies and favorite foods can be tabulated and shared with the cook. Information such as parents' work addresses and hours, each family doctor's name and address, and the guardian if parents are not available should also be organized and readily accessible.

Parent Groups

A nucleus of motivated parents can be an enormous resource in involving parents who are reluctant to be active. Parent-to-parent interaction is often less threatening than parent-to-teacher approach. Once they observe the success of the team effort, less motivated parents will reach out to the warmth and emotionally satisfying results of this dynamic relationship. Initially some less motivated parents may view the cohesiveness between the responsive parents and the teachers as the in-group. Early childhood educators need to accept these responses, yet continue to invite these parents to various activities. In some cases, a one-to-one approach may work. Here again, involved parents can help. Teachers can identify friendship patterns among the children's families and use these friendship patterns to involve other parents in selected events. This may break the initial resistance and bring some of the parents into the parent-teacher partnership. Some hesitant parents may have specific needs that, if identified, may be tactfully addressed by the parent-teacher group.

Another way of communicating with the parents is through parents' meetings. These meetings may be social or educational in nature. In social meetings, families have an opportunity to get acquainted with each other and develop close friendships and support systems. During educational meetings, parents have specific goals and expectations and will need an agenda to keep the group moving and accomplish what they want to.

The early childhood educator needs to make sure the parents are aware of meeting times. Several possible meeting times may be selected by parents and then one or two of those time slots used to accommodate different schedules. For example, if parents choose Saturday mornings and an evening during the week, some meetings can be held on Saturday mornings and others during the week evening, allowing both groups of parents to participate. The format and structure for the meeting should be developed by the group and then adhered to. The early childhood educator may need to adjust the staff schedule in order to use that time for parents' meeting, and ask one teacher to be responsible for each group. The teachers involved can then share notes and ideas with each other and maintain communication between the groups. Each group should have about six months to work together before any major changes are made in the group. In addition to their other group activities, parents should be encouraged to evaluate their satisfactions, dissatisfactions, and accomplishments with the parental involvement programs so they can refocus their attention toward the future. Each group needs to examine the reasons for the successes and failures and make specific suggestions for future improvement. It may be useful to invite administrators to some of the social and educational meetings of parent groups, and we educators also need to examine our performance within the group to develop insights in our own strengths and limitations. Thus the social and educational meetings will be conducted in harmony with the goals and growth we desire in the parental involvement programs and with the children. Study and work groups can also emerge out of the larger groups as parents and teachers with specific interests come together.

Informal Contacts

Most early childhood teachers may find that the beginning of the school day presents opportunities for informal contact with parents as they bring their children to school, provided the teacher plans carefully and sets up before the children arrive. Similarly, the end of the day also presents potential for exchange of ideas if the parents are not tired, rushed, or preoccupied. If they are not, a pleasant conversation can occur. Teachers should be available to all parents coming in and may need to plan the facilities carefully to provide this accessibility. A pot of coffee and disposable cups may help build rapport with some parents, as will active listening, undivided attention, and genuine interest. Such encounters act as door openers, helping teachers become aware of parental concerns, needs, and interests around which parental involvement may occur. Some of this knowledge may echo our own needs and concerns, producing a basis for involving parents.

We also need to capitalize on our encounters with parents at the supermarket, church, park, or restaurant. Since these opportunities occur away from the school setting, they show parents the human side of the teachers, not just the professional side.

Brief personal notes to parents also provide meaningful personal communication between parents and early childhood educators. A simple way of acquiring data for these notes can be an anecdotal notebook maintained in each classroom. Whenever an interesting episode takes place during the day, respective teachers jot down brief comments about it. Short personal notes carrying some of these events provide a unique dimension to parent-teacher relationship because they indicate the educator's personal concern and involvement with the child.

Knowledge of these episodes is particularly meaningful to parents who are away from their children for long hours because of their jobs.

Phone calls are useful in providing personal contact with the parents. These calls are specially appreciated when there is illness or a new birth in the family. These indications of concern for the families of the children help parents reach out, ask for assistance, or share a concern with early childhood educators.

Newsletters

Newsletters are an effective way of presenting a variety of information to parents. They can provide information about the curriculum activities for the month, school menus, school closings, and other information related to the program of the school. Newsletters can also share specific suggestions for learning experiences that parents may follow at home with their children. Most newsletters include educational information covering topics that appeal to most parents, such as behavior-management, ideas for a rainy day, preparing children for the arrival of a new sibling, nutrition, sibling rivalry, and television pros and cons. Suggestions for specific topics can be solicited from the parents, while other topics may be selected by the early childhood educators. For example, during spring an article regarding poisonous plants may be appropriate. Ideas for outdoor play during the summer may be timely, or the parents may appreciate occasional articles discussing the selection of play materials. No matter what the topic, the article should be readable, brief, and practical, giving specific suggestions to the parents. Children's art work and comments add an extra touch of humor and life to the newsletter. Favorite recipes, review of books for children and parents, and community events of interest are useful additions, as is an idea exchange column for the parents to contribute to.

Bulletin Board

A parent's bulletin board can be an indispensable addition for parental involvement if it is conveniently and conspicuously located. The bulletin board can provide a brief overview of children's daily activities, give pertinent announcements, and relay messages between parents and teachers or among parents. Some of these notes may be about birthday parties, visits to each other's houses during weekends, or confirmations of social plans among families. Some early childhood programs like to use a portion of the bulletin board for "Gems of the Day," some of the cute comments and antics of the children.

Shared School Time

Open-door policy in early childhood programs provides for additional motivation and communication; each program can experiment with different ideas and define its own policy. Some programs allow parents to walk into the classroom any time they want. Others set up specific times during which parents and visitors are permitted to participate. Lunch time can be very useful as an open hour, particularly if parents can pay a small fee to the school and eat with their children. In such cases, reservations should be requested at least twenty-four hours beforehand to insure that adequate amounts of food are prepared. Many early childhood programs prefer parents to visit during the free play periods. This allows opportunities for visitors to move around the classrooms and observe the children without distracting them from structured play.

Parents can also be involved in the learning experiences of children. For example, if one of the themes during the school year is "People and Their Jobs," parents can come and share information about their occupations. Such involvement will require flexibility from the teachers to accommodate parents' work schedules and will provide a brief inservice training for the parents involved, but the result is well worth the effort. Mother's or Father's Day can be celebrated by inviting parents to participate during the appropriate weeks. All of these strategies will help build the type of teamwork and exchange that will make parental involvement viable and valuable.

Summary

Educators must understand that parental involvement is a process and not a product. It will take time, energy, and commitment to make the process work for both parents and teachers and help provide optimum development for the children. Yet parents and teachers can help each other fulfill their responsibilities, while bringing home and school together with new respect, concern, and sensitivity toward each other.

References

Bloom, B. S. 1981. *All our children learning.* New York: McGraw-Hill Book Company.

Gordin, I. 1972. *Child learning through child play.* New York: St. Martin's Press.

———. 1975. *The infant experience.* Columbus, Ohio: Charles E. Merrill.

Hayakawa, S. I. 1963. *Symbol, status, & personality.* New York: Harcourt, Brace and World.

Honig, A. S. and Lally, J. R. 1981. *Infant caregiving: a design for training.* Syracuse: Syracuse University Press.

Hymes, J. 1974. *Effective home-school relations.* Sierra Madre: Southern California Association for the Education of Young Children.

Johnston, M. 1980. Parents & children: mutual resources in the development of self-esteem. Paper read at Annual Conference of Midwest Association for the Education of Young Children, April at Milwaukee, WI.

———. 1981. Designing learning environment for the decade of the 80's: challenges for teachers and parents. Paper read at Annual Conference of Midwest Association for the Education of Young Children, April at Rochester, MN.

Kenniston, K. 1977. *All our children: the American family under pressure.* New York: Harcourt, Brace, Jovanovich.

Pierce, J. P. 1972. Communication. *Scientific American.* 3:31–41.

White, B. 1979. Developing a sense of competence in young children. In *Families Today.* N.I.M.H. Science Monograph. 1:865–878.

———. 1975. *First three years of life.* New York: Prentice-Hall.

Working with Difficult Parents

Richard D. Rundall and Steven Lynn Smith

Richard D. Rundall has devoted his professional career to programs in early-childhood development. He has been director of a nursery school in Illinois, consultant at a child-parent center, and teacher at a child-development center. At present he is a training consultant for Project RHISE/Outreach at Children's Development Center in Rockford, Illinois.

Steven Lynn Smith has been staff psychologist at the Montana Center for Handicapped Children at Billings and training coordinator at Project RHISE/Outreach, where he is now project director. With Richard Rundall he is coauthoring a publication assessing learning capabilities of young children for the Illinois State Board of Education. The two have also pooled their resources to produce this article dealing with ways teachers may encourage reluctant parents to cooperate in helping educate their young children.

The writing of this article was supported in part by Grant No. G008100731 from Special Education Programs, U.S. Department of Education. The content does not necessarily reflect the position or policy of that agency and no official endorsement should be inferred.

Since the necessity for parental involvement in early childhood programs has been widely recognized, the predominate question today is not whether to involve parents, but how to involve them. Many innovative programs provide opportunities for involvement. As a result, parents are no longer limited to the more traditional methods of involvement—fund raising, being "educated" about child development topics, and being updated on their child's progress. Parents are now seen as valuable allies in promoting their child's development; in planning, administering, and evaluating the program; and in informing the general public about program services. Early childhood programs that not only recognize the many roles parents can fill but also offer parents a variety of opportunities usually see a significant increase in participation among the parents they serve.

There are, however, some parents who seem to ignore any efforts to reach them. There are some parents who, no matter what extra efforts are made by the staff, are unwilling to even attend a program function. Other parents cooperate in some ways but in other areas appear to be very unreasonable, uncooperative, or seem to lack understanding of the importance of some of our concerns or suggestions. There is, in fact, a wide range of parents who are "difficult" to work with or to get involved in our programs.

In this article we will discuss techniques and strategies that can be used to help involve these kinds of parents more in early childhood programs. The first part of the article will focus on what appears to be the most difficult parents to work with—abusive and neglectful parents. We will discuss who these parents are, why they are this way, and how we can help them. Later in the article we will focus on more general techniques for working with a variety of "difficult" or reluctant parents.

Who These "Unreachable" Parents Are

Unreachable parents are often called by other names: multi-problem families, hard-core families, or multi-agency families. We recognize these families by the difficulty we have working with them. Some seem apathetic; some seem limited in their understanding of child development and children's needs; some seem to lack basic parenting skills; some are resistive or hostile to our attempts to involve them. Some are even critical of us. These parents fail to attend meetings, fail to keep appointments, fail to get their child to the program on a regular basis, and fail to benefit from any of our efforts to reach them. Usually they either drop out of the program or are dropped from program services.

We can also recognize these difficult families by the anger, frustration, and feelings of impotence and failure we experience when we try to work with them. We think they don't care, that they are unreachable, that they don't want help. "Why should I waste my time when there are so many other families who need our help and who appreciate it?" And if we really think about it, that is the real heart of the issue. That is why we drop "unreachable" parents from our

client lists, why we terminate services—not because the parents are unreachable, but because we feel we can't reach them. And we don't like
that feeling. We don't like to be reminded by their names on our client
list that we have failed to involve them. We don't like to be reminded
by each missed appointment or by their lack of follow through that we
have made another unsuccessful effort to involve them.

It is much easier to drop these parents from our rolls—to see them as
uncaring, to blame them for not becoming involved in the program—
than to feel that we failed in our efforts to reach them. But we can take
some relief from the fact that this "blaming" process is not unique to
early childhood programs. William Ryan (1971) explains this as a rather
common occurrence in our society. He feels the process of attaching
blame follows three steps. First, we identify a problem. Then we study
those affected by the problem and discover how they are different from
the rest of us as a consequence of deprivation and injustice. Finally, we
define those differences as the cause of the problem, which shifts the
blame from us to them.

Thus, in early childhood programs we identify the parents as not
being involved, look at their apparent lack of knowledge and limited
skills, and define them as "unreachable."

Unfortunately, in early childhood programs we do not have the option of labeling parents "unreachable" and blaming them for not being
involved in their child's program. Research by Gordon, Bronfenbrenner,
and Lazar have all documented the importance of parental involvement
in programs serving young handicapped children, children of low income families, and children who risk abuse and neglect. The research is
quite clear. If we want to effect a lasting change in the child's development, the parents must be actively involved in their child's program.
We cannot, therefore, allow ourselves to define the parents' inability to
make use of our skills and knowledge as their problem. We cannot
blame the parents. The problem is not that all of these parents are unreachable, but that we have not yet been able to reach them.

While there are some parents who really are unreachable no matter
how much we try, no matter how much extra effort we put forth, there
are many who can be involved if we can define the problem as our inability to reach them rather than their inability to benefit from our efforts, if we can understand why they appear to be unreachable, and if
we can understand what it takes to reach them.

With more appropriate expectations—based on the parents' needs
and readiness for involvement—we will be more likely to try to involve
parents in ways that they are ready for and able to respond to.

Why They Are "Unreachable"

Dr. Ray Helfer (1975, 1978) has identified those parents we view as
unreachable as adults who missed childhood, who are products of a

cycle of abnormal parenting. In other words, they are children of people who were also difficult parents. He calls this cycle the World of Abnormal Rearing (WAR cycle). The WAR cycle as Helfer conceives of it is essentially a situation in which children who never had their needs met grew up physically but not socially and emotionally. They have, in fact, missed their childhood. As grown-ups with children of their own, they spend their parenthood years attempting to have their lost needs met by their children and, as a result, raise children whose needs are also never met. A brief review of the cycle explained by Helfer will clarify this further.

Conception, Pregnancy, Child

WAR cycle parents usually want their children because they feel the child will resolve their problems, provide them with the love they do not have, and meet their needs. The baby, of course, is unable to do this.

Unrealistic Expectations, Role Reversal, and Compliance

These parents generally have unrealistic expectations of the child. Since that little girl cannot meet these expectations, she then becomes a scapegoat, "can never do anything right," and is constantly chastised, belittled, neglected, or abused.

Often a role reversal situation occurs in which a child "takes care" of mom and dad and assumes responsibilities around the house that are entirely inappropriate for her age level. These parents expect the child to do for them what they wish their mother had done when they were small, and so the child is not allowed to act like a child.

Lack of Trust, Isolation, and Low Self-Esteem

As a result of the unusual manner in which the child is raised, she does not develop the ability to trust. She feels responsible for her parents' problems and fails to recognize the supportive role others can play in her life. She becomes isolated; she can't help and will not be helped. Eventually she develops a conviction that she is no good.

Selecting "Friends" and Mates

As these children reach adolescence, they feel that their experiences at home and school with parents and friends have been negative. Their inability to select friends is also manifested in their choice of mates, a choice often influenced by a desire to leave home and find someone to meet their needs. Since the mate turns out to be unhelpful and unsupporting, the goal of the relationship quickly becomes having a baby, and the cycle begins over again.

Childhood Missed

WAR children spend so much time trying to meet the needs of their parents that they miss their own childhood because the more the child acts like a child the less likely he will be accepted in the family. Most opt for skipping childhood. This causes a significant gap in their developmental process; and since experiencing childhood is a prerequisite to mature adulthood and parenting, these children perpetuate the lifestyle their parents have fostered.

Although Helfer became aware of the WAR cycle while working with abusive and neglectful families, we need to recognize that all people who are products of the WAR cycle do not fit our typical picture of the abusive or neglectful family. Some of these families have positions of status in the community. They are, on the surface, a family that appears stable. But the parents' ability to recognize and meet their child's needs is as limited as the family across town who was reported for abusing their child. These parents, like the more easily identified abusive and neglectful parents, can be recognized by the following kinds of characteristics, commonly cited in the literature on abuse and neglect (DHEW 75-30074; Polansky, Desaix, and Sharlin 1977):

- immaturity and dependence
- a sense of personal incompetence
- difficulty in experiencing pleasure
- social isolation
- misperceptions of the child
- fear of "spoiling" the child
- belief in the value of punishment
- unawareness of the child's needs.

To fully realize the impact of the WAR cycle on the parents' ability to be involved, it is important that we first recognize the impact such a cycle of parenting had on them as young children. Studies of abused and neglected children indicate a group of common developmental problems that appear in these children significantly more often than in the normal population (Green 1978; Martin 1976). These characteristics include difficulty relating to another person, and in establishing trust, inability to enjoy play or show pleasure, a poor self-image, preoccupation with many fears, delays in speech maturation and difficulty verbalizing feelings, lack of exploratory activities, slowness in development without sufficient neurological explanation, and school learning problems.

Studies reported in a recent DHEW publication, *Child Abuse and Developmental Disabilities: Essays,* indicate that there is a close relationship between abuse and neglect and developmental disabilities. One study indicated as high as 70 percent correlation between abused children and those who are perceived as developmentally different by parents.

The real nature of the impact of this inappropriate parenting cycle on the young child is explained in detail by Harold P. Martin and Martha Rodeleffer in a chapter titled "Learning and Intelligence," in *The Abused Child*. The authors describe the early environment of the child as creating impediments to learning (development) rather than as stimulating or promoting learning. These psychosocial impediments include an unpredictable, non-nurturing world; restricted learning opportunities; inadequate stimulation and support; danger in both performing and not performing; all learning energy channeled into survival; and anxiety.

An Unpredictable, Non-nurturing World

In the normal home, parents respond to a child's needs. When the child is upset or uncomfortable, the parent reacts and helps resolve distress. As a result, the child begins to associate pleasure with the parent and learns that she can cause change. The world becomes predictable. When the parent does not recognize the child's needs and these needs go unmet for extended periods of time, the child's world makes little sense. With no order or structure, it is unpredictable.

Restricted Learning Opportunities

In the normal home environment the child has opportunities to explore, to play, and thus to learn. In the home where the parent is preoccupied with her own needs, the child is given little opportunity to explore or play. He may be kept in one room of the house or in a crib or playpen. In some instances his natural exploration of the environment may be viewed as "getting into things" or "messing up the house." In either case, significant sensory, motor, and cognitive deprivation can occur.

Inadequate Stimulation and Support

In the normal home a child has support for his development. The parent provides opportunities that are generally appropriate to the child's readiness to achieve them and verbally supports the child's efforts with encouragement, reinforcement, and corrective feedback. Verbal interaction itself is valued. When the opposite occurs—when there is no encouragement or reinforcement and when corrective feedback is essentially negative responses to the child's inability to do or say the right thing—it is easy to see how the child may begin to function less fully than he is capable of or may begin to lose some of the enjoyment of learning and of interacting with adults.

Danger of Performance and Nonperformance

Normally children are encouraged to do what they are capable of doing. Expectations are generally appropriate to their skills and developmental level. It is easy to understand the dilemma a child is faced with, however, when he is routinely confronted with pressure to do something he is developmentally unable to do and punished for not being able to meet the parents' expectations. The situation becomes more complicated for the child when the parent also punishes him for refusing to try that which he knows he cannot achieve.

Energies Preempted by Survival

In the normal home a child's energies are spent in playing, interacting with others, and in other growth producing and pleasurable activities. In the home we have been describing, the child's energies are spent in survival activities. He must continually be sensitive to his environment and especially to his parents. He develops the ability to read moods since he may be ignored, punished, praised, or laughed at at different times. His moral development excludes right or wrong behaviors that most children normally develop and incorporates the mood of the adult as a way to judge whether his behavior is acceptable or unacceptable. Most of his energy is directed toward obtaining love and approval of the parents. These children also manifest role-reversal. They become the parents' comforter, sensitive to the parents' feelings and moods, and responding to the parents as we would normally expect the parent to respond to a child.

Anxiety

A child in a normal home will at times experience anxiety in response to events in his environment. The child in a WAR cycle experiences significant amounts of anxiety on a continual, daily basis. This anxiety, a physiological response to his daily environment, has a dramatic impact on his ability to learn, play, and interact with his peers and adults.

Even with only this brief overview it is apparent that children reared in the WAR cycle lack the nurturing and stimulating environment that is the foundation for most children's cognitive, motor, social, and emotional development.

What then is the answer to helping the parents we come in contact with who are victims of such abnormal parenting themselves? What can we do for an adult who has experienced this abusive cycle as a child? How can we counteract the years of negative influence and break the cycle? The answer is much simpler than we might think.

How These Parents Can Be Helped

Most people who work with young children are familiar with Erik Erikson's "Eight Ages of Man." Erikson (1963) explained that these eight psychosocial stages of ego development are part of the process by which all persons establish basic orientations to themselves and their social world. He proposed that each stage had a positive and a negative component and that these stages were critical steps "of decision between progression and regression, integration and retardation." Each stage is psychosocial strength that is symmetrically related to all others; all of them depend on the proper development of each one in the proper sequences. Erikson (1961) further developed this theory to include the virtues of man, the "specifically human qualities of strength" which he felt were "imported from generation to generation." He felt that man's survival had depended upon these virtues being developed "in the interplay of successive and overlapping generations." The specific virtues which he felt began to develop in childhood were hope, will, purpose, and competence.

If we examine closely the virtues Erikson identified and consider the implications of their absence in someone's life, we can recognize the true nature of the effects the abnormal rearing cycle has had on the parents we work with. Without hope; without self-control or willpower; without a sense of purpose; and without a sense of competence to begin, follow through with, and complete a task, parents cannot become involved in a program just because we expect them to do it. If we examine our relationship to these parents, we find that we are often continuing the abnormal cycle their parents used on them and they are using on their own children. This can be more easily demonstrated by examining some of our attitudes toward them.

Often we have unrealistic expectations of them. We usually expect the parents to understand the necessity for and to want to be involved in our programs. We expect them to recognize their child's needs, to respond to those needs, and to postpone some immediate gratification of their own needs. In other words, we expect them to be mature, caring, nurturing individuals when they cannot.

We lack empathy, finding it very difficult to understand why the parents do not recognize the necessity for involvement, why they do not seem to care for their child, and why they then fail to respond to our promptings, urgings, and requests.

In a type of role-reversal, we want these parents to recognize the importance of what we can do for them and their child. We expect them to tell us how we have helped them, how significant we have been in their lives, and how much they appreciate our efforts to help them.

Also, we believe in harsh punishment. If parents will not cooperate with us or become involved in the program, we usually want to drop them and replace them with someone who is cooperative.

Unfortunately, these typical attitudes are counterproductive to our efforts to reach the parents. Therefore, the first task in reaching the unreachable parents is to examine our own attitudes and feelings. We must be prepared to accept the parents as they are and to offer them, not what we need in the way of their involvement in our program or what their child needs in the way of parenting, but what the parents themselves need to grow. What these parents need from us, what they never received from their parents, is nurturing. They need to be accepted for what they are, encouraged for what they've done, reinforced for their efforts, and, finally, they need to feel understood.

Our major focus with these parents must be on developing a nurturing relationship based on trust and self-esteem. All efforts and actions on our part should be carefully evaluated on this basis: will this facilitate trust between us and will this promote the parents' self-esteem? We cannot hope to make any lasting progress with the parent until a trust is firmly established or until the parent begins to feel good about himself. These are keys to change and growth because with the ability to trust and with increased self-esteem (autonomy) will come the virtues hope and willpower. Hope for the future and the willpower to act on that hope are essential to the parents' ability to take advantage of the help we have to offer them.

In order for us to achieve this type of relationship and to do an effective job of building their self-esteem, we must recognize that there will be many things about the parents and the parents' relationship to the child that need to be changed but that we must ignore for a time while we establish a relationship. Unless the child is in immediate danger of injury or illness or unless the neglect is significant enough to report, we need to accept their unacceptable behavior. This is extremely important because confronting a parent early in the relationship or "sharing a concern" with them will break what trust is already established and will lower the parents' self-esteem.

How We Help Ourselves Help Parents

The role we assume in establishing a relationship with parents is one that recognizes we are the instrument for change. We use ourselves to nurture and assist another person so that person can change and grow. This is a lengthy process; we should expect it to take place only over a period of time, only by having many face-to-face and telephone contacts with the parents. We should also expect that this will be a frustrating process for us at times. It is not uncommon to feel angry, depressed, helpless, or ready to give up on the parent.

In order to deal with these feelings as they arise, we must insure that a support system is in place to help us. This support system could include our supervisor, a colleague, a formally established regular meeting in the program to discuss problem cases, or a regular meeting with a mental health or social service consultant. Any of these alternatives allows the opportunity to recognize, vent, and control the feelings that will normally arise while we use ourselves as instruments of change with unreachable parents. If we do not take steps to deal with these feelings, either they will push us into the "blaming the victim" cycle or they will interfere with our ability to establish a relationship with the parent.

At times it may even be important to deal with the physical symptoms that usually occur with these feelings. The tension and anxiety that accompany anger, depression, helplessness, and hopelessness should be eliminated in some way. Jogging or some other form of exercise, hot baths, cleaning the house, and rearranging the furniture are all positive ways of decreasing physical symptoms. Changes in eating habits, sleeping patterns, smoking, or use of alcohol—though temporary solutions—are not healthy, long-term solutions for tension reduction.

Another factor to consider in working with unreachable parents is that often when you feel the relationship is finally established, an apparent setback will occur. Children who have faithfully attended the program will be absent for no apparent reason, or the parent will not be at home for a prearranged home visit. Efforts to reinvolve the parent seem to fail. This is especially frustrating after our previous success in reaching the parent. When this happens, it is usually because parents recognize they are becoming close to you. They are afraid of this new, trusting relationship, or they feel they are not worth liking or caring about; so they test you and the relationship. "Will she really like me if she sees how bad or unlikable I am? Does she really care about me, or is she here because I am cooperating?" At this time it is extremely important to preserve and continue every effort. Generally, if we can weather this storm, the relationship with the parent will be securely established. This is a time to rely heavily on a support system and to use our stress-reduction activities. If we can maintain our calm, accepting, non-threatening, nonconfronting attitudes with the parents, the relationship will be firmly established. Then we will be able to begin to sensitively guide the parents, promote their understanding of their child, and to change their behavior.

In summary then, the formula for reaching unreachable parents is to establish a relationship with them that will develop trust and self-esteem; recognize that you are the instrument of change as you play a nurturing role with the parents. While doing this, ignore minor concerns, maintain patience, expect a testing of the relationship, and make sure to develop a support system for yourself.

Specific Techniques for Establishing a Relationship

Many specific techniques can be used to promote the relationship, some examples of which will be given here. However, because all parents are different, all relationships are unique. Since you are the tool of change, and developing a relationship is a process, no single step-by-step approach can be used with every parent. You must decide what to do from moment to moment to establish the relationship by analyzing the situation at that point in time and determining what techniques to use and when to use them to match the needs of the relationship and the parent. *Child Abuse and Neglect: The Problem and Its Management, Vol. 2* provides an excellent overview of parents' needs you may have to meet.

- The parents need help to feel good about themselves to compensate for the devastating belittling they have experienced through their lives.
- They need to be comforted when they hurt, supported when they feel weak, and liked for their likable qualities.
- They need someone they can trust and lean on, who will be on time for appointments, will be there in times of crisis, and will put up with their crankiness and complaining.
- They need someone who will not be tricked into accepting their low sense of self-worth.
- They need someone who will not be exhausted with them when they find no pleasure in life and when they defeat all attempts to help them experience pleasure.
- They need someone who can help them meet their practical needs, either by directing them to appropriate resources or by providing more direct help.
- They need someone who understands their difficulty in having dependents when they themselves have never been able to be dependent.
- They need someone who will not criticize them, even when they ask for criticism, and who will not tell them how to manage their lives.
- They need someone who will help them understand their children without making them feel either called upon to understand what they cannot or stupid for not having already understood.
- They need someone who can give to them without making them feel inadequate for their need to be given to.
- They need someone who does not need to use them in any way.
- They need to feel valuable. Eventually, they need to be able to help themselves and to have some role in helping others.

In establishing a relationship with these parents, remember that the child's needs must come second to the needs of the parents. This may cause some mixed feelings as we watch the child's needs go unmet by the parent, but we must continually remind ourselves that only through establishing a trusting relationship can we improve the parents' under-standing of and interaction with the child.

Techniques must be devised that take these various needs into ac-count and fulfill them, and that we feel comfortable using. If we create or try a technique with which we feel uncomfortable, the parent will recognize our feelings and will believe that our discomfort is with them, a belief that will impede rather than assist developing a relationship.

Some of the techniques that others have successfully used to help es-tablish a relationship with an unreachable parent are listed below:

• Identify the parent's strengths and reinforce their efforts.

• Provide a service for them. Many of these parents have never had anyone wait on them or care for them. Serving them a cup of coffee can be a way of saying "I care for you. You are worthwhile."

• Set realistic, concrete goals. Short term, attainable goals established with the parent's involvement can show him that you can help him and that he can succeed.

• Prepare the parent for the unknown. Explaining what is going to hap-pen, what you are going to do, and what will be expected of him helps reduce the fear of new, unknown experiences. This is especially true of situations where you will not be present.

• Communicate on a superficial level. Talk about external things at a concrete level rather than personal, abstract issues. This is much less threatening to parents and will enable a relationship to be established much more quickly.

• Focus discussion and conversation on the parent, his concerns, inter-ests, and difficulties. Too much attention on the child will cause some parents to feel a competition for your attention.

• Assign separate staff to the parent and the child. This will also help eliminate the parent's need to compete with the child for the staff member's attention.

• Be consistent. Consistency and predictability in the relationship will promote trust. Honesty is also important since if the parent feels that he has been lied to, the relationship will be destroyed.

• Advocate for the parents. Referrals for needed services or assistance by another agency can enable the parent to see you as a source of help to them. They may also need you as an advocate to ensure that they re-ceive the services.

• Use photographs. Many parents do not have pictures of their chil-dren. Taking pictures of them playing with or holding their child can reinforce pleasurable time spent with the child.

While you are utilizing these and other techniques to establish a rela-tionship with an "unreachable" parent, remain fully aware of the true nature of that relationship. We are, in reality, creating a dependent relationship, usually viewed by most people as unprofessional. It is true that a dependent relationship is unprofessional if the dependence is based on the needs of the professional. If, on the other hand, the only way to assist the parent to change is through establishing a trusting relationship and providing the nurturing (reparenting) he never had as a child, we should expect that a normal result will create some dependence. It is, in fact, not only to be expected but rather to be looked for as a measure of how real that relationship is. Ways in which we recognize this is happening are that the parent relies upon us or counsels with us about decisions he must make. He will spend more time talking about his problems or feelings. He will telephone us even after office hours and will initiate an increased number of unscheduled face-to-face contacts. The parent may also recommend us as a resource to other people.

When those things happen, they are usually trying experiences for us, but we must remember the importance of that dependency in solidifying the relationship. Once the parent is dependent upon the relationship, we can gradually begin to set limits and make demands of him that would have frightened him away before the relationship was secure. In addition, as soon as we realize the dependency is established, we must also begin to work the parents away from that dependency. We must teach them to use the relationship (and us) in a less dependent, more mature fashion and assist them to develop a support network of existing friends and relatives. If they do not have the necessary friends, we might also introduce them to new friends through parent-to-parent matches or socially oriented parent groups.

Unexpected telephone calls and unscheduled visits by the parent can be difficult to deal with. At times the staff member must be able to have messages taken rather than take the call or to have the parent told that the staff member is unavailable to meet at that time. A receptionist or secretary who is trained to handle phone calls and face-to-face contacts with stressful or impatient parents can assist us in establishing a relationship with parents. The secretary should be trained to understand the special needs of these parents while remaining warm and patient. If we must postpone contact or a phone conversation with the parent, later we should share the reason for this, whether it was because of another commitment or because we were exhausted after a tiring day and could not face another unexpected visit. Most parents will be able to understand how difficult it is to concentrate on their concerns if the staff person is in a bad mood. We should feel that it is acceptable, at times, to say no to a parent's demands and not feel guilty. No one can be expected to continually respond to unexpected requests. Attempts to do so will create even more stress on the relationship. By the sensitive nature of the effort required to nurture parents, an increased need exists for staff members to draw upon their own support mechanisms and methods of reducing the physical symptoms of tension.

All people who choose to make the effort to reach unreachable parents should be extremely careful about recognizing their own and the program's limitations. One staff person should not try to work with too many of these parents at any one time because of the extra energy required for a successful job. A tendency exists in organizations to identify a staff member who is effective and to give that person all the difficult families. But the amount of energy required to carry a full caseload of parents who need special efforts is beyond what most individuals have to offer.

Additionally, research indicates that programs designed to reach these families are not always successful. For this reason it will become necessary, at times, to make a decision about whether to stop providing services to a particular parent. This decision, although unpleasant, may be necessary because of the staff member's continued special efforts, other families that need to be served, and an indication that the relationship is not developing. However, the decision to drop or stop service to a parent should not be made lightly or alone. A supervisor, colleagues, or a consultant should assist in the process. If the decision is made, the parent must be informed personally, if possible, but if not, then by mail. He should never be made to feel guilty and should never be blamed for his inability to take advantage of the services we offer. An opportunity may arise at a later date when he is ready for assistance or has been referred by an authority (social services or doctor), and this termination experience should not prevent him from coming back. The parent should be told that the staff person recognizes there were pressures in his life that made it difficult for him to use the services, but if at a future time he feels those pressures are resolved and would like to use the services offered, he can contact us. This will insure that we do not place an additional burden on an already fragile self-esteem and that the parent will feel that our agency accepted and understood him. Usually, if he is again referred to our agency or contacts us for services, he will be much easier to involve in the program.

Other Patterns of Maladaptive Parenting

The most recognizable of the maladaptive parenting patterns are the emotionally or socially abusive and neglectful parents we have discussed. The techniques described previously are all useful in establishing a relationship with these parents. There are, however, several other maladaptive parenting patterns that require some different expectations and efforts on our parts.

Psychotic Parents

Although some psychotic parents are abusive or neglectful, not all of them are. If the parent is on medication or the psychosis is in remission, the parent may be able to be involved in the child's program. Our role with these parents is to offer them opportunities for involvement while at the same time being sensitive to possible symptoms of the problem. These parents' needs are usually beyond establishing trust, support, and encouragement. Our role is to facilitate their involvement with mental health/psychiatric services or to encourage their continued involvement if they are already receiving services. If we cannot encourage their use of professional help, we should recognize our limitations. We must simply be prepared for sporadic attendance, questionable behavior, mood swings, and irrational thoughts. We must also be prepared for regression in the parents' behavior or in their involvement in the program. By maintaining flexible expectations for psychotic parents we can offer them maximum opportunity for involvement with a minimum of unrealistic pressure.

Alcoholic Parents or Drug-Abusing Parents

Another type of parent who we must recognize as beyond our normal ability to help is the alcoholic or drug-abusing parent. While we should continue to offer these parents opportunities to be involved in the program, we must realize we are not able fully to meet their unique needs and should direct some of our efforts toward securing professional treatment for them. The parent may, of course, choose not to be involved with professional services. But unless he becomes disruptive, he should not be excluded from the normal opportunities for involvement. Rather, our expectations should be adjusted to expect some inconsistent, inappropriate, and unpredictable behavior. At times a parent may be involved and at other times he may avoid us. There may be significant mood swings from depression to highs. If we recognize that this is normal behavior for an alcoholic or a drug-abusing parent, we may accept more easily whatever amount of involvement the parent is capable of.

Hostile Parents

Parents who are hostile, critical, or resistive are especially frustrating to work with; these can include both the unreachable parents we have already described as well as other parents who may be cooperative or involved in some other ways. The first step in dealing with these parents is to analyze the situation carefully. Is this really hostility or resistance, or is the parent motivated by a genuine concern for her child and questioning something about the services, exercising a healthy self-assertion. In other words, if the parent truly has a point or misunderstands, we should not define it as criticism, resistance, or hostility. Instead we need to deal with it in an objective manner. It may be also that the parent is not accustomed to being assertive or expressing concerns and does this in a way that appears to be more hostile than he intends.

Some parents who appear to be hostile may be reacting to the realization that their child is handicapped or has developmental problems. We should be careful to recognize this as a possible reason for what may appear to be irrational anger. The grieving process parents experience is a normal, natural reaction and is, in fact, necessary in helping to cope with a devastating discovery. These parents need to be allowed the opportunity to ventilate. They need to be accepted, listened to, and told that their anger is normal. If you find yourself in a situation in which a parent is expressing hostility or criticism, the following guidelines are useful:

• Accept the anger and concern. Reflect understanding of the parent's point of view.

• Listen for reasons behind her anger or concern. Sometimes parents are unable to say what is really bothering them, but by listening, you can help them eventually get to their concern (sometimes the emotion behind anger is fear or feeling threatened).

• Remain composed. Do not let the parents' behavior make you angry. Fight the tendency to get excited, and make yourself talk slowly and softly.

• Give the parent feedback regarding her anger or concern. By letting her know you recognize her feelings you can sometimes eliminate her need to show that feeling.

• Do not retreat from anger. Angry people often sense fear in people, and this reinforces their use of the anger. Showing them you are not afraid by remaining calm and composed can sometimes prevent increasing anger.

• Do nothing to threaten her or make her feel she has to fear you. It is important to stay in control of body language.

• Maintain a positive attitude. It is difficult for a person to be angry if you maintain a positive attitude toward her.

• Accept and validate the parent's concerns, and abandon any pressure to get her to be rational.

• Leave in a calm, composed manner. Make it clear that the conversation is ended and that you will get back to her in the near future.

While experiences like this are certainly not enjoyable, when we work in the helping and educating professions, we encounter situations like this. But we should not let this deter us from continuing to work with people.

Confronting Parents

Dealing with and confronting parents on sensitive issues is a difficult task. When we work with reluctant parents, it is even more difficult.

This section will provide guidelines for knowing both when and how to confront parents on almost any issue.

First, make sure you have established a relationship with the parents. Confronting parents prior to establishing a relationship will usually interfere with the relationship rather than resolve the concern. Also, find out about the family's dynamics. Is this a real concern or a normal habit for the family that will have no internal negative or derogatory effects? Sound out a professional peer or a supervisor regarding your decision to confront. This can help you decide if confronting is best for the client and not a reflection of your need to ventilate.

Next, examine whether you're emotionally ready to confront the parents. If you have not resolved your feelings enough to discuss the issue in a calm manner, don't try. If you have had a particularly bad day you may want to postpone plans for confronting a parent that afternoon.

Once you are there, deal with only one issue. Confronting must be done in such a way that the parents feel you care. The situation must not be used as an opportunity to dump all your concerns on the parent. Use either the sandwich technique or the seed planting technique to actually share your concern with the parent. Realize that a commitment is being made to care. Even if the parents reject your advice you must continue to work with them.

After you have confronted a parent, realize that you are responsible for follow-up. The parent may be hurt or angry, so it is up to you to make the next contact and show that there is a continuing commitment to the relationship. (If the parent responds with anger or hostility, use the techniques suggested for dealing with hostile parents.) Remember that honesty and concern are two-way processes. The parent may begin to share concerns with you, and you need to be ready to accept this and reinforce it.

As mentioned, the two techniques to use when confronting a parent are the sandwich technique and the seed planting technique.

Sandwich Technique

When approaching parents with this technique we are offering them a verbal sandwich—the meat of the problem between two slices of bread from their interests and concerns.

Bread: I know how much you care about Johnny and that you do not want him to be hurt or unhappy. Because I know you care so much for him I knew you would want to know this.

Meat: The problem is that some days when he comes to school some of the other children make fun of him and tell him he stinks. He is terribly hurt by this and usually cries.

Bread: I know you don't want him to be hurt. How do you think we can help him so he is not hurt again?

Seed Planting

When you use the seed planting technique you are planting the seed of the problem, but eliminating the need for an immediate discussion about the problem. This bypasses some of the defensiveness which normally arises and allows the parents to discuss it when they have had some time to think about it.

The seed: Mrs. Jones, I have noticed that Mary has been absent several times frequently, and I'd like to get together sometime to discuss this with you. I know I caught you unexpectedly and you're not really ready right now to think about how we can help her get here more often. Maybe we could talk about it next week on Thursday or Friday.

These two techniques can also be combined:

Jane, I know how much you want Tommy to do well here at school. You've shared with me before that you want him to have a successful experience this year. I knew you'd want to know if something might prevent that from happening. That's why I thought it was important to tell you that he can hardly pay attention to the lesson. I know if we get together and talk about it sometime, we'll be able to figure out a way to help him. Maybe next week we can get together and think this through. I'll call you Tuesday and we can set up a time.

Whichever technique you choose to use, it must be used in a way that respects the parents, allows them the right of helping solve the problem, and accepts their inability to fully act on your information or change if they are unable to at the time. If we can do this, confronting them will not destroy our relationship, and we will find that, at times, we can successfully promote change in the parent.

Individualizing for Parent Needs

Throughout this article we have discussed several general types or categories of parents in order to help us better understand how to involve them in our programs. Each parent is a unique individual with special needs and wants. None of us would think of working with a child unless we knew something about him. In fact, it is a relatively common practice to formally assess young children to determine where they are functioning developmentally, what their needs are, and what their learning style is. Unfortunately, when the child enters the program, it is a relatively infrequent practice for the parents to be assessed. We tend to expect that they all will not only benefit from but will want to be a part of the services we choose to offer them.

When we notify parents of a parent meeting, we expect all parents to be interested in this topic because *we* feel they should know more about it. When most of the parents do not attend, we become upset. A far more practical method is to assess the parents' interest in a specific topic and expect only that those who are interested or need that information will attend the meeting.

We could assess other areas besides parents' interest in topics for a parent group, such as whether the parents' interest in a topic should be met by a group experience, by individual parent-to-parent discussion, by staff-to-staff discussion, or by providing the parent with written materials. Additional areas of parental assessment that should be considered are counseling needs, volunteer interests, and parental knowledge and skills.

We should wait until we have established a relationship with the parents before using formal methods of assessment. Assessments that are conducted too early may not provide valid information and may also frighten off the parents because they do not yet trust us. We should, therefore, use informal observation and recognition of needs at first, postponing the formal assessment process until the relationship is firmly established.

Home visits can be used to get a view of the parent-child relationship in a natural setting. They can also provide us with an awareness of the ecological stresses the family faces in their daily living. Home visits can help establish trust as well, since parents may be pleased that we care enough to come to their home. Some parents, however, may not want us to see their home, and we should be flexible enough to recognize when a parent is putting us off or avoiding our efforts to make a home visit. In that case, we may want to arrange to visit in some other relaxed setting outside our agency.

Summary

Many of the parents we have thought were unreachable are able to be reached if we change our attitudes toward them and our expectations of them. We must never assume because of a parent's behavior that they do not care or that they are incapable of becoming involved in our program. Instead, we should always ask, "What gets in the way of their doing what is appropriate? What prevents them from taking advantage of what we are offering? What do they need to help them to become involved?" And we must remember that anyone can tolerate parents who are tolerable. If we want to reach reluctant parents, we must learn not only to tolerate those whose behavior seems intolerable, but also accept, understand, appreciate, and nurture them—not because we need them to be involved in our program but because this is the way to insure the maximum and most lasting growth for their children. Because we care about all children and want what is best for them, we must be willing to give of ourselves and make special efforts to reach parents that, in the past, we would have given up on because they were "unreachable."

The key, then, to involving parents in our programs is to recognize each one as a unique human being and to understand, as much as possible, their needs, the dynamics of their family relationships, and their family lifestyles. In this way we will be able to offer parents services they will be able to take advantage of, and we will have appropriate expectations for their level of involvement in our program.

References

Briggs, R. R. 1979. *Child abuse and developmental disabilities: essays.* DHE Publication No. (OHOS) 79-30226.

Bronfenbrenner, U. 1975. Is early intervention effective. In *Handbook of Evaluation Research,* vol. 2. Beverly Hills: Sage Publications.

Dept. of Health, Education, and Welfare. *Child abuse and neglect: the problem and its management,* vol. 2. DHEW Publication No. (OHD) 75-30074.

Erikson, E. H. 1963. *Childhood and society.* New York: W. W. Norton and Company, Inc.

Erikson, E. H. 1961. The roots of virtue. In the *Humanist Frame,* ed. J. Huxley. New York: Harper and Brothers.

Gordon, I. J. 1970. *Parent involvement in compensatory education.* Urbana, IL: University of Illinois Press.

Green, A. H. 1978. Psychopathology of abused children. *Journal of Child Psychiatry* 17:92–110.

Helfer, R. E. 1975. *Child abuse and neglect: the diagnostic process and treatment programs.* DHEW Publication No. (OHD) 75-69.

————. 1978. *Childhood comes first.* East Lansing: Ray E. Helfer.

Lazar, I. 1981. Early intervention is effective. *Educational Leadership* Jan: 303–305.

Martin, H. P., ed. 1976. *The abused child.* Cambridge: Ballinger Publishing Company.

Polansky, N. A., Desaix, C., and Sharlin, S. A. 1977. *Child neglect: understanding and reaching the parent.* New York: Child Welfare League of America, Inc.

Ryan, W. 1971. *Blaming the victim.* New York: Random House.

Part 2
Involving Parents in
Specific Areas of Education

Parents and the Child's Search for Self

Jean M. Larsen

Jean M. Larsen is associate professor and coordinator of early childhood education at Brigham Young University. With an undergraduate degree in elementary education and a Master of Science in child development, Dr. Larsen received her Ph.D. in educational psychology at the University of Utah. She has conducted research into parent-child relationships and has written papers, articles, and manuals on the subject. Dr. Larsen is past president of the Utah Association for the Education of Young Children.

It is generally recognized that a positive self-concept is basic to all aspects of development and learning, yet all too often we find children who are not developing healthy self-concepts. Since professionals seem to agree that an individual is not born with a self-concept (Combs et al. 1974, Felker 1974, Levy 1972), it is logical to assume that the self-concept emerges through experience and interaction with significant others. If we find, then, that a young child shows indications of a potentially low or negative self-concept, we may speculate that the experiences and interactions provided for that child in the home setting have not been conducive to promoting a positive self-concept. Because the self-concept continually changes, the self is highly flexible and responsive to environmental conditions. As stated by Combs et al. (1974), "We learn that we are men and women able or unable, acceptable or unacceptable, liked or unliked, depending on the kinds of experiences we have had in the process of growing up. Once established, the concept we have of ourselves continues to affect our behavior, perhaps even for life" (pp. 17–18).

Feelings About Self Result from Parent/Child Interaction in the Early Years

Two factors seem to be predominant in the creation of a positive self-concept: the age of the child and the interaction skills of parents. The preschool years are important in self-concept development. As indicated by Stenner and Katzenmeyer (1976), the beginning school years (ages five to eleven) make up the period in which the child's self-concept crystallizes. A great deal has been contributed to this development prior to the crystallization period; therefore, as substantiated by many professionals (Felker 1974, Jersild et al. 1975, Kagan 1971, Stenner and Katzenmeyer 1976), the first six years of a child's life are crucial years in a child's self-concept development.

Stott (1974) suggests that if that little boy is to develop positive feelings about himself, he must have the experience of being regarded positively by those who matter most in his life. What people can give that child a feeling of self-worth better than his parents, especially since the child's view of acceptance is based on the degree to which he believes his parents value him? As Coopersmith (1967) has said, we value ourselves as we are valued.

During children's early years, parents play a most significant role as the main teachers of their children. According to Kagan (1971), the child's parents are the most important social influence on his psychological development. The child identifies with his parents because they are the adults he knows best and whom he admires and respects. It is through his parents that a child learns to feel a sense of belonging and worth.

That little girl develops a sense of competence and accomplishment as parents create opportunities for successful experiences and then provide a confirmation of the child's value and worth through verbal and physical expressions of love. Dinkmeyer and McKay (1976) further emphasize the potential effects of more positive parental interaction skills by suggesting that a parent indeed can help build a child's confidence and feelings of worth through the use of encouraging statements that include valuing and accepting the child as she is, pointing out the positive aspects of her behavior, expressing appreciation for effort and improvement, and showing faith in her so that she can come to believe in herself.

Not only is it important for parents and other significant adults to use positive statements of encouragement with the young child but also to assist the child's verbalization of positive self-relevant language, such as

"I can do it" and helping her to attach positive meanings to verbal symbols. It has become apparent that one of the best ways to teach a child to use positive self-statements is in the context of natural parent/child interactions.

Before continuing this discussion of the importance of parent/child interaction and ways to initiate positive self-regard we will identify the various components of self-concept and establish their relationship to development in the young child.

The Self-Concept

Often the terms *self-concept, self-esteem,* and *self-worth* are used interchangeably. Some professionals claim that self-concept refers to physical make-up and appearance, personal attitudes, perceptions, values, relationships, and opinions that a person holds about himself (Rogers 1959, Snygg 1949, Yamamoto 1972, Allport 1961, Perkins 1965). Other writers indicate that self-esteem results from how one views himself, how others view him (friends, family and peers), and how well he can perform in comparison with others (Dinkmeyer 1965, Branden 1969, O'Connell and O'Connell 1974, Yonemura 1968). With some caution, then, we may say self-concept refers to an individual's idea of who he is, while self-esteem becomes subsumed in the self-concept as the worth or value dimension.

McCandless (1967) further defines self-concept as "a set of expectancies, plus evaluations of the areas or behaviors with reference to which these expectations are held." As an individual accumulates a repertoire of experiences in a given area, he begins to formulate ideas or perceptions of what he is "really" like, and thereby develops a greater awareness of his abilities and attributes.

Years ago in Portland, Oregon, as an unseasoned but enthusiastic beginning teacher, I was assigned a first grade in a new school that serviced a rapidly developing middle-income residential community at the outer limits of the city. Because there were still problems of school boundaries to be worked out, on the first day of school I was confronted with forty-six bright yet bewildered six-year-olds; that is, forty-five six-year-olds and one not yet five who had slipped in with the confusion. I had been notified at the outset, by both parents and the previous kindergarten teacher, that Sam was subject to violent temper tantrums. Pamela would cry because her mother was not allowed to remain with her, and Tom was so precociously inquisitive I should keep all gadgets out of his reach in order to prevent his disassembling or breaking them. And there was Marie, who was very accident prone and should be guarded. When we were assembled on the rug for our first reading of the "Biggest Bear," Pam started to cry for her mother; Tom proudly presented me with a handful of metal pieces that had once been a pocket watch and said, "Look, teacher, the 'motor' fell out"; and Sam arched his back and started banging his head on the floor. At that moment, the teacher from the next room appeared at the door to notify me that Marie had just smashed two fingers in the restroom door and needed attention. In desperation, I shrieked for everyone to be quiet and not to move or breathe. Then clumsily I tried to take care of each crisis.

The expectations of the behaviors of each of these children had been clearly predicted, and they responded accordingly. Each was contributing to what has been designated as a history of experience from which future expected behaviors are derived and that add to the building of one's self-concept.

Influencing Self-Concept Potential

Many professionals (Klausmeier and Goodwin 1975, Felsenthal 1972, Bernard and Huckins 1971, Coopersmith 1967, Brownfain 1952) have described the self-concept as "positive" or "negative" and potentially "high" or "low." The descriptive term *potential* has been incorporated to denote the emerging, fluctuating, or changing self-concept. Realizing the use of the words *high, low, positive,* or *negative* with the term *self-concept* implies an evaluative dimension (identified earlier as self-esteem), I use this evaluation in describing the broader term self-concept.

A person with a positive self-concept is self-assured, confident, happy, vibrant, and energetic (Felsenthal 1972, Coopersmith 1967) and thus recognizes his abilities and attributes and is able to demonstrate competence. Brownfain (1952) asserts that a person with a stable self-concept is well adjusted, accepts himself as he is, values himself, and is free of nervousness and feelings of inferiority. This kind of person is well liked, considered popular by the group, and sees himself as he believes other people see him. He feels secure about himself, and when he asks himself the question "Who am I?" he can answer in a confident manner and is usually pleased with his answer. He feels worthy, lovable, and significant, and he acts with competence and confidence (Bernard and Huckins 1971, Klausmeier and Goodwin 1975, Brownfain 1952).

An individual with a potentially high self-concept is eager to learn, believes he is capable of learning, and has confidence in his own abilities. He recognizes his talents and abilities without trying to outdo others, can feel regret or remorse without being burdened with guilt, and has no need to pretend to be someone he is not.

A person with a positive, stable self-concept responds emotionally to himself and others. This type of individual sees enough difference between the real self and the ideal self (the image he has of the person he would like to be) to serve as motivation for self-improvement; yet he feels like a desirable being.

On the other hand, a person with a negative or potentially low self-concept feels insignificant, unworthy of being liked, unloved, incompetent and futile (Bernard and Huckins 1971), and has feelings of depression, shame, or guilt (Coopersmith 1967). If this individual's performance does not match his personal aspirations, he regards himself as inferior no matter how high his attainments. He concludes his achievements are of little importance, and unless he can reach his desired goals, he views himself as unsuccessful and unworthy. A person with a low self-concept has higher levels of anxiety and emits a low frequency of positive self-statements (Hauserman, Miller, and Bond 1976).

Becoming aware of or recognizing what constitutes a positive self-concept is preliminary to the more arduous tasks of assessing potential level and then insuring that the majority of experiences in which the young child is engaged produce success.

Components of the Self-Concept

For the purpose of gaining insight into the components of the self-concept, let us identify what I have defined as three "experience" categories. Note that each area is not clearly dichotomized, but rather interfaces with others. *Emotional state* is the label of the first dimension, or behavior area. Experience situations representing both ends of the continuum of this component include feelings of happiness, sadness, contentment, anger, security, anxiety, fearfulness, ecstasy, misery, and uneasiness. While it is true that the reality of living produces both negative and positive experiences, we should insure that young children especially are not continually exposed to an overproportion of negative situations. Teachers of young children can and do provide an appreciable number of daily activities that benefit a child's sense of emotional stability. Similarly, the home setting can offer an atmosphere conducive to a pleasant or contented emotional state. Indeed, children have a greater tendency to be happy rather than unhappy. But this tendency can be lost very quickly if parents and teachers do not make a deliberate effort to avert such a tragedy.

Recently a father expressed his concerns about his seven-year-old daughter. He related that as a toddler at two, and on to three and four years of age, this child had been almost "too precious" to describe. She seemed to be bubbling over with happiness and warmth. She was able to attract attention and admiration from everyone. Now, at seven, she is exactly the opposite. Most of the time she is extremely unhappy, her vivaciousness and enthusiasm for life very dim. The sadness and unresponsiveness of this once vibrant child gives cause for her parents' concern.

The obvious question is "What happened to create such a change?" It need not have been a traumatic experience or even a major crisis that effected this complete turnabout. Perhaps it was subtle changes in the child's physical features caused by the growth process; or perhaps it was her adjustment (or lack of adjustment) to expected behavior. Very often without a deliberate attempt to do so, parents or significant others cut off positive verbal feedback and start sending the type of messages that cause a child to evaluate her "self" differently, creating unhappy or uncomfortable feelings. A child needs to be accepted as an individual no matter the stage of growth or the child's interests.

Skill competence is the second component contributing to the self-concept. Aspects of this area relate to an individual's perceived ability to do—both physically and intellectually. Experiences include problem solving, asking and answering questions or obtaining and giving information and ideas, manipulating toys and the self in motor skills, fulfilling routine chores, and many other task-completion activities. Skill development is of great importance to the young child. Ability to *do* is essential to a positive self-concept. Every child should have the opportunity to experience success or achievement in at least one area. Again, ample opportunity exists for teachers and especially parents of young children to provide experiences that will result in skill development.

This component may be better illustrated with two personal examples of efforts to enhance skills and their results. When our boys were very young, beginning at about the time they were two and five years of age, we made it a practice to play number games as we were riding in the car, waiting for doctor appointments, or preparing to go to bed. Over a period of time, both boys became very proficient at counting, then at adding and subtracting series of numbers, and eventually at abstract problem solving. By the time our second boy was six or seven he could arrive at the sum of purchases at the store (including tax) before the clerk had them rung up on the cash register. This skill provided a source of satisfaction, not only for him but for his parents. As he grows older, his competence with math continues to be a dominant aspect of his concept of self.

The second example concerns our daughter's motor-skill deficiency. In a conference with her kindergarten teacher we were told our daughter was "doing as well as could be expected under the circumstances—not being able to skip, catch a ball, nor jump rope very well." Needless to say, we as parents were dismayed that our "pride and joy" was failing "P.E." in kindergarten. We determined that perhaps her deficiency was compounded by the fact that neither of her parents had expertise in the physical-skill area. Thus we began immediately to obtain assistance from people who had such competencies to tutor our child, to provide some degree of success in this very crucial area of development. Now as a teenager she has a degree of competence in several motor skills.

The third dimension, or component, of the self-concept deals with *behavior* (appropriate actions), primarily pertaining to social interaction—getting along with others. This area, again identifying both ends of the continuum, includes perceived acceptance, preference for interacting with peers, and ability to relate to significant adults, along with gregariousness, shyness, destructive aggressiveness, "naughtiness," acts of sharing, taking turns, and showing concern for others.

A number of years ago I had an opportunity to work with an unusual group of five-year-olds. These children were so well endowed with abilities and attributes that our experience together provided many beautiful examples of children's social competence. One afternoon out on the play yard Debbie and Amy had placed two large wooden crates against the play yard wall and were standing on them in order to observe the construction of the new library on the other side of the wall. As the two girls strutted back and forth on their improvised reviewing stand, they made comments about the operation of the large construction machinery. Soon they noted Becky coming to join them. Both Amy and Debbie spread out their legs and arms and taunted, "Becky, you can't come up here—we're here." Becky backed away for a moment, then taking a firm stance and looking squarely at the two girls with her hands on her hips, very precisely announced, "Amy and Debbie, Heavenly Father sent us here to share—now please move over; I'm coming up." Amy and Debbie glanced at each other with an "Oh, then that's all right" expression and quickly moved over to make a place for Becky. It is evident that even at the age of four or five years, individuals can engage in associations that contribute greatly to either building or limiting social competence.

These three dimensions: emotional state, competence (in cognitive and motor skills), and (social) behavior are those I have determined to be the more significant components of the self-concept. Experiences with young children have further led me to believe that parents can create settings conducive to enhancing each of these dimensions.

Parents Have Responsibility for Early Learning

During the past two decades while child-development professionals have placed heavy emphasis upon early learning and the value of preschool education programs, my views on these matters have made a rather significant shift. Twenty years ago when I began training teachers of young children, I was convinced that the lives of most three-, four-, and five-year-old children would be greatly enhanced through attendance in a "good" preschool program. Indeed I looked to a preschool group experience as the answer to many educational and social problems in today's society. This idealistic view has been somewhat altered by the realization that even the most enriched group environment, for a brief two-hour period of time (or even an eight-hour education and care situation) does not usually combat the extended experience with parents and family in the home. However, if the group experiences become supplemental to that which is occurring in the home, the ultimate positive effects are evidenced.

Therefore, I now look at the real value of the preschool group experience to be directly related to or contingent upon the degree to which the preschool program motivates parents to fulfill their responsibility as the main educators of young children. Let me hasten to say that I still view the early group experiences as beneficial but not ultimate in their outcomes.

With this increased recognition that both the home and school environments have a significant bearing upon children's motivation, achievement, and learning, many educators have accepted the need to establish home–school partnerships. The development of this home–school partnership requires not only changes in each of the separate institutions but also changes in their interaction. The focus of this change might best be directed toward the home–learning situation and the relationship among home, school, and community rather than on the classroom instructional process.

As creators of the home environment, parents become the first and most important teachers of children. However, parents come from a variety of backgrounds and many are unprepared to effectively teach their children. As Ira Gordon (1975) suggests, some parents lack any notion that they are or should be "*teachers*" of their young children. Because of their lack of prior training or the deficiency of on-the-job training, it is no wonder that many parents have not developed the abilities to teach their children.

One of the greatest challenges of our time, then, is to teach parents that they are capable of teaching their young children effectively and that their home can be a learning resource. One roadblock that must be overcome is the idea of society in general, and many professional educators in particular, that "real" education begins when school begins. Parents and educational institutions share joint responsibility and should have a common goal to help all children achieve their greatest potential. However, the bulk of the responsibility must belong to the parents, for children attend the home school for two decades or more.

Fortunately, some parents are beginning to be motivated to improve their parenting skills and to become more effective teachers of their children. A recent report (Lazar and Darlington 1978) on the long-term effects of Head Start programs over the past fifteen years indicates that some of the earliest compensatory programs for poor children have had lasting benefits—especially those that focus on the interaction between parent and child.

Effects of Parental Involvement

David P. Weikart and Lawrence J. Schweinhart, codirectors of High/Scope Educational Research Foundation, have been studying the long-range effects of preschool education as well as various aspects of parental involvement. Recently the results of their definitive study concerned with the overall impact of attending preschool upon later adjustment to society have been announced. This study, called the Perry Preschool Project, has followed the lives of 123 disadvantaged black children from preschool age to the present (over an eighteen-year period).

On forty-eight measures of school and life success, the study shows that by age fifteen, children who had attended a quality preschool significantly outperformed children who had not. These findings offer the strongest evidence to date that preschool education can have very extensive positive ramifications for those who attend. Weikart and Schweinhart have determined from their research that one of several significant factors related to the outcome was the substantial involvement of parents in the child's education. The motivation for parental involvement was stimulated by weekly home visits of preschool teachers.

An earlier research project sponsored by High/Scope was a pilot study conducted in 1966 to explore home teaching as a means of providing preschool services. Building on the experience of the home teaching component of the Perry Project, the mother was seen as the major force in the education of her young child. The program included thirty-five children and their mothers in the experimental group and twenty-nine in the control group. Weekly home visits were provided for four months. The basic problems under investigation were to determine the acceptability by mothers of "home teaching only" as an alternative to a combination of home teaching and preschool classes, and to discover the impact of "home teaching only" on the intellectual development of a sample of disadvantaged four-year-olds. The findings from the project indicated that mothers would accept home teaching; indeed, they were enthusiastic about it, and 91 percent of all home visits were completed as planned. Cognitive data collected on project children showed that the experimental children significantly outperformed the control children on general intellectual ability (Weikart, 1979).

A third study, the Ypsilanti-Carnegie Infant Education Project (Lambie et al. 1974), was one of the first home-based preventive education programs for disadvantaged infants. Sixty-five families participated. Infants entered the project at three, seven, or eleven months of age and were randomly assigned to one of three "treatments" (experimental, contrast, control). The experimental treatment consisted of weekly home visits with mothers and infants by trained educators over a sixteen-month period and intensive observation and testing. The contrast treatment consisted of weekly home visits by untrained women from the community and the same testing schedule as the experimental group. Families in the control group received the same testing as families in the other groups but no treatment. The results of the project indicate that the children in the experimental group consistently, though not always significantly, scored higher on measures of intellectual ability and displayed better language development than the children in the other two groups.

Another interesting series of studies reported in the *Carnegie Quarterly* (1979) are being conducted by Phyllis Levenstein and her staff at the Verbal Interaction Project (VIP) in Freeport, Long Island, New York. One of these projects, entitled the Mother-Child Home Program (MCHP), incorporated conceptual capacity curiosity, social readiness, and relationship with parents—in order to preserve children's native intelligence and equip them to take advantage of school. Twice a week, from fall through spring, a VIP-trained "toy demonstrator" visits a participating mother and her youngster at home, bringing with her a bagful of toys, picture books, and puzzles that are rich in "concept categories." The home visitor pulls out a different, more complex item each week and plays with the child *and* the mother for about twenty minutes, all the while engaging them in conversation that is interesting and fun for both. At the end of the session she departs, leaving the item behind as a gift.

The process that seems simple to an observer is in fact very subtle. The home visitor does not teach or counsel, but "models" verbally interactive techniques. For instance, she encourages the youngster to name and think about the features of the toy or book—its colors, shape, size, texture, relationships (up, down, next to, under), number, what causes things to happen, classes of things. The mother, noting what she does, begins with her child between sessions. "Once she sees she has an effect, that her child is learning," says Levenstein, "our experience is that she will continue the interactive behavior no matter how burdened she is by circumstances." And because the play is carried out in a way that praises the child for doing well and ignores lapses, that encourages curiosity, imagination, and independence, it tends to make learning exciting and anxiety-free. The child's relationship with the mother is strengthened as a result. Indeed, learning takes place, according to Levenstein, partly because the child is in the relationship.

Follow-up studies have indicated long-term positive effects upon the children who had this enriched early experience. At the end of the third grade, mean I.Q. scores of the children who had participated in the MCHP were not only higher than the control group who had not had home intervention but were also higher than the national average (*Carnegie Quarterly* 1979).

After surveying numerous intervention programs—some of which included parent participation and others without parent involvement—Bronfenbrenner (1974) postulated the following deductions:

The evidence indicated that the family is the most effective and economical system for fostering and sustaining the development of the child. The evidence indicated further that the involvement of the child's family as an active participant is critical to the success of any intervention program. Without such family involvement, any effects of intervention, at least in the cognitive sphere, are likely to be ephemeral, to appear to erode rapidly once the program ends. In contrast, the involvement of the parents as partners in the enterprise provides an ongoing program while it is in operation, and helps to sustain them after the program ends (p. 55).

Ways to Enhance Parental Teaching and Interaction Skills

In response to the finding regarding the positive outcome of parental involvement with their young children and also because of the desire many parents have to be more effective teachers of their children, a variety of parent education models and services have been developed to foster such parental teaching skills.

Brigham Young University Preschool/Parent Education Program

A parent training program has been developed at Brigham Young University in connection with the early childhood education and child-development laboratories. This program has been established not only to assist parents in becoming better teachers of their own children, but also to train prospective early childhood educators in the parent-education dimension. Currently some 200 sets of parents are participating in this program, which offers five options as to how they will be trained.

The enrollment in the nursery program is contingent upon the parents' willingness to participate in parent education. They may select from the following participation options: audio tapes, home visits, group lectures, readings, and assisting in the preschool laboratory. The content information for the various topics is controlled across the five options.

While a number of research projects have been conducted or are in process directly related to the parent-education program, the general intent of two studies has been to investigate the effectiveness of this program in assisting parents to develop and apply teaching skills with their own children.

Self-Concept Enhancement in the Home Setting

Another variation of the Brigham Young University parent-education approach is a program specifically designed to assist self-concept development of young children in the home setting (Vance 1980, Mifflin 1980). This program has been directed to parents whose preschool-age children demonstrated a potentially low self-concept level. Four- and five-year-old children were screened (by means of the Early Childhood Self-Concept test) and from all children attending the Brigham Young University preschool and children enrolled in the Mountainland Head Start program in Utah County.

After children with potentially low self-concept levels were identified, their parents were contacted and invited to attend a series of four parent-enrichment workshops. Because parents of the children attending the University preschool were required to participate in parent education, their attendance was expected. However, the Head Start parents did not have the same requirement but were encouraged by their program director to attend the workshops. It was gratifying, therefore, when most of the Head Start parents contacted became enthusiastic participants in this program. Forty children and their parents were involved in the project. The parents received suggestions for appropriate activities to promote an awareness of their own attributes and abilities. The materials presented to parents in the workshops were based on the following five-point rationale:

1. Parents are the first and most important teachers of their child.
2. A person is not born with a self-concept; it emerges through experiences and interactions with significant others.
3. A child needs to feel a sense of belonging, competence, and worth.
4. A vital part of self-concept development consists of teaching the child to use positive self-referent language such as "I can do it" and helping him to attach positive meanings to verbal symbols.
5. Parents are encouraged to help the child feel worthy.

Parents who participated in the training workshops demonstrated an increased ability to provide statements of positive verbal support and encouragement. In addition, there was some indication that the enhanced skill of the parents had a positive effect on the children's self-concept level.

Mother Enrichment: A Home Demonstration Program

In an effort to further deal with the growing need for better parental interaction and teaching skills, the Mother Enrichment Program has been conceived (Larsen, in press). The purpose of this functional program is two-fold:

1. To assist parents in establishing positive relationships with very young children, relationships based upon greater understanding of children's needs and abilities.
2. To show mothers how to capitalize upon play experiences in the home and to teach their children—beginning in infancy and following through the very crucial years of early childhood.

I emphasize at the outset that it is not intended such intervention will remedy or solve serious family problems. The goal of this program is to avert problems by assisting parents to develop the necessary skills to better fulfill their responsibilities as the first and most important teachers of their young children and thereby experience greater satisfaction in the parent role.

The Mother Enrichment Program was designed to be implemented through the existing network of visiting teachers in the Relief Society (the women's organization of the Church of Jesus Christ of Latter-day Saints). The program, which attempts to involve mother and child in brief, frequent, and positive play/learning activities through several effective parental teaching procedures, is taken into the homes of families with children from birth through five years—at the request of the mothers.

The visiting teachers, who have been trained by a specialist to demonstrate positive behavior patterns and teaching procedures, take a toy, play material, or an activity appropriate for the age and show the mother how to use it with her child. Visiting teachers do not merely explain the teaching procedures or the game, they actually become engaged in the activity with the child. Then the mother interacts with the child as she has been shown, with the visiting teachers as observers. When needed, the visiting teachers also provide information on child care and developmental characteristics of children.

A key to the success of the program is the selection, training, and functioning of a ward mother-enrichment specialist. The primary role of the specialist is to act as a resource person and trainer for the visiting teachers. A set of self-training materials helps prepare the mother enrichment specialist for this crucial role. These materials include a guide book and a training workbook with audiotape instructions.

This enrichment program has been implemented with mothers of young children in the Brigham Young University community. An assessment of the program's effects gave support for this approach as a way of assisting mothers, especially young, inexperienced mothers, to be more effective at interacting with and teaching their young children.

Parental Expansion of Classroom Learning

A final example of a project designed to assist in the development of parental teaching and interaction skills has been conducted in connection with a public school kindergarten in Price, Utah. The general purpose of this project was to establish and evaluate a parent-teacher involvement model designed to enhance learning of kindergarten children. This purpose was accomplished by teaching teachers how to deliver to parents basic information about learning processes, parental influences, and child development.

According to program developers, the use of parents as facilitators of their child's learning is assumed to be of maximum benefit when both parents are involved. Consequently, this project attempted the involvement of both fathers and mothers as stimulators of their child's attitude toward learning. The response of fathers, many of them truck drivers or coal miners, was beyond expectation.

At a recent conference, four families representative of those participating in the kindergarten project were invited to demonstrate some things they typically do in a home learning activity session. In addition, the parents were asked to give a brief response as to their feelings about the program.

Each family took about five minutes for the demonstration. One father showed how he had taught his child (with mother and younger children joining in) about signs of spring and started off with a song, "Popcorn Popping on the Apricot Tree." Another family had a number game that was the basis of their favorite activity; another read a story with rhyming words, then made up their own word-rhyming game; and still another family was involved in a follow-the-directions game.

After the demonstrations, in the response session, one of the fathers said that this program had helped him to better understand the learning level of his daughter. He said he had been so disappointed when at the beginning of school he wrote out a page of simple addition and subtraction problems for her to do and she couldn't do one of them. Now he knew that his expectations had been too high and he understood better the kinds of things that are more appropriate for his child.

When asked what changes in their teaching skills they had experienced as a result of the kindergarten program, some of the responses from parents were the following:

"We have developed more patience with the kids and listen closer to the things they are saying."

"We enjoy describing and helping the children understand about things in our world."

"In trying to spend more time with the children, I have grown closer to them. I feel better about myself as a mother; consequently, I am happier and easier to get along with."

"I watch him more when he is playing or talking with his brothers."

"Both of us listened to our daughter more and we have taken more time with her when she wants to talk with us."

Summary

Each of the programs described has demonstrated functional ways parents have been assisted in better fulfilling a teaching role with their child's search for self. These programs are representative of those that have successfully incorporated some basic guidelines in order to further parental effectiveness. The following statements summarize these guidelines:

• Parents are the first and most important teachers of young children.

• In young children, learning occurs more readily in the natural environment.

• The early years are crucial for developing positive concepts about self.

• Most parents have neither the skill nor the confidence to interact with and teach their children as effectively as they would like.

• Parents can be helped to enhance their teaching skills and to utilize the routines of the home in providing meaningful learning experiences.

• The relationship parents establish with their child from the beginning and their continual involvement in the educative process are the major factors affecting the development of that child's positive self-concept and his or her ultimate success in life.

References

Allport, G. W. 1961. *Pattern and growth in personality.* New York: Holt, Rhinehart and Winston, pp. 128–30.

Bernard, H. W. and Huckins, W. C. 1971. *Dynamics of personal adjustment.* Boston: Holbrook Press.

Branden, N. 1969. *The psychology of self-esteem; a new concept of man's psychological nature.* Los Angeles: Nash Publishing.

Bronfenbrenner, U. 1974. *Is early intervention effective? A report on longitudinal evaluations of preschool programs,* vol. 2. Washington, D.C.: Office of Child Development, United States Department of Health, Education, and Welfare.

Brownfain, J. J. 1952. Stability of the self-concept as a dimension of personality. *Journal of Abnormal and Social Psychology* 47:597–606.

Cahoon, Owen W. and Olson, Terrace D. 1978. *A model of parent-teacher involvement to enhance learning in kindergarten children.* An unpublished report presented to Follow-Through, Department of Health and Human Services, Washington, D.C.

Carnegie Quarterly vol. 27, no. 1. 1979.

Combs, A. W.; Blume, R. A.; Newman, A. J.; and Wass, H. L. 1974. *The professional education of teachers.* 2d ed. Boston: Allyn and Bacon.

Coopersmith, S. 1967. *The antecedents of self-esteem.* San Francisco: W. H. Freeman.

Dinkmeyer, D. C. 1965. *Child development: the emerging self.* Englewood Cliffs, New Jersey: Prentice-Hall.

Dinkmeyer, D. and McKay, G. D. 1976. *Parent's handbook: systematic training for effective parenting.* Minn.: American Guidance Service.

Felker, D. W. 1974. *Building positive self-concepts.* Minneapolis: Burgess Publishing Company.

Felsenthal, H. 1972. The developing self: the parental role. In *The child and his image,* ed. K. Yamamoto, pp. 178–203. Boston: Houghton Mifflin.

Gordon, I. J. 1975. *Human development: a transactional perspective.* New York: Harper & Row.

Hauserman, N., Miller, J. S., and Bond, F. T. 1976. A behavioral approach to changing self-concept in elementary school children. *The Pychological Record* 26: 111–16.

Jersild, A. T., Telford, C. W., and Sawrey, J. M. 1975. *Child psychology.* 7th ed. Englewood Cliffs, New Jersey: Prentice-Hall.

Kagan, J. 1971. *Personality development.* New York: Harcourt Brace Jovanovich.

Klausmeier, H. J. and Goodwin, W. 1975. *Learning and human abilities: educational psychology.* New York: Harper & Row.

Lambie, Dolores Z., Bond, James T., and Weikart, David P. 1974. *Home teaching with mothers and infants.* The Ypsilanti-Carnegie Infant Education Project: An Experiment. Ypsilanti, Michigan: High/Scope Education Research Foundation.

Larsen, Jean M. (In press.) *Mother enrichment: the development and evaluation of a home instruction program.* Accepted for publication in *Family Perspective.*

Lazar, Irving, and Darlington, Richard B. 1978. *Lasting effects after preschool.* Summary Report. DHEW publication no. OHDS 80-30179. U.S. Government Printing Office, Washington, D.C.

Levy, R. B. 1972. *Self-revelation through relationships.* Englewood Cliffs, New Jersey: Prentice-Hall.

McCandless, Boyd R. 1967. *Child behavior and development.* New York: Holt, Rhinehart and Winston.

Mifflin, Ruth Egelund. 1980. Enhancing parental teaching and interaction skills with young children. Unpublished Master's Thesis, Brigham Young University.

O'Connell, V., and O'Connell, A. 1974. *Choice and change.* Englewood Cliffs, New Jersey: Prentice-Hall.

Perkins, H. V. 1965. Changing perceptions of self. *The self in growth, teaching, and learning,* ed. D. E. Hamachek, pp. 449–53. Englewood Cliffs, New Jersey: Prentice-Hall.

Rogers, C. R. 1959. A theory of therapy, personality and interpersonal relationships as developed in the client-centered framework. In *Psychology: a study of science,* vol. 3, ed. S. Koch, pp. 184–256. New York: McGraw-Hill.

Snygg, D., and Combs, A. W. 1949. *Individual behavior.* New York: Harper and Row.

Stenner, A. J., and Katzenmeyer, W. G. 1976. Self-concept development in young children. *Phi Delta Kappan* 58:356–57.

Stott, L. H. 1974. *The psychology of human development.* New York: Holt, Rinehart and Winston.

Vance, O. Jean. 1980. *The effects of parental assistance upon young children's self-concept development.* Unpublished Master's Thesis, Brigham Young University.

Weikart, David P. 1974–75. Parental involvement through home teaching. Annual Report. Ypsilanti, Michigan: High Scope Educational Research Foundation. Reprinted in *Readings in early childhood education 78–79: annual editions.*

Yamamoto, K. 1972. *The child and his image.* Boston: Houghton-Mifflin.

Yonemura, M. 1968. Supervision in early childhood education. *Young Children* 24:104–109.

Parents and the Reading Process

Doris K. Williams

Doris K. Williams is professor and coordinator of home economics graduate studies at Bowling Green State University. She has published two books, several journal articles, and miscellaneous newsletters and pamphlets on subjects dealing with educational psychology and child development. Dr. Williams has conducted extensive research in early-childhood education.

The Parental Role

Parental involvement in the educational process is beneficial to children. That involvement is especially significant in the process of learning to read (Howard 1972; Cook 1975).

Researchers tell us that children do better in school when they perceive parental interest and involvement in their education (Spadefore 1979). Experiments to develop better parent-teacher rapport have resulted in "children's significantly increased levels of self-esteem, motivation to learn, improved academic attitudes, and higher levels of reading achievement." Other studies have concluded that parental involvement in the learning process helps children develop respect for school, individual, and property rights, as well as an improved self-image that enhances reading achievement (Larrick 1976; Rich 1976).

Getting parents involved in the learning-to-read process can occur at two basic levels. First, local school with district-wide community involvement programs and parent training courses offered through a school district's adult education program are useful on a large-scale basis. Second, at the individual level, teachers need to encourage parents to take an interest in what is happening at school. The outstanding teacher will assume the responsibility for encouraging parents and children to talk about what happens in school, review homework together, and discuss the kinds of learning taking place.

A number of school administrators are taking seriously the research that has shown the value of parental involvement in the total learning process. In Houston, Texas, for example, school officials developed a program called "Operation Fail-Safe" (Riouz 1980). When the project began in the fall of 1978, nearly three-fourths of Houston's parents with public school children turned out for highly publicized individual conferences with teachers to discuss the children's basic abilities and achievements, along with ways parents could help promote reading skills. Parents received computer lists of suggested readings and simple activities for their children to complete at home after school. (More information about this particular project can be obtained from the Superintendent's Office, 3830 Richmond Avenue, Houston, Texas 77027 [Riouz 1980]. Information about a similar project, the Wisconsin Design for Reading Skill Development, upon which "Operation Fail-Safe" was based, is available from National Computer Systems, 4401 W. 76th Street, Minneapolis, Minn. 55435.)

In another experiment in Chicago, students, parents, teachers, and principals signed contracts, making certain commitments to further the education process. Through "Operation Higher Achievement," parents promised to give their children wholesome food and appropriate clothing, to encourage their children by reading to them, and to insist that they spend time studying. The students promised to "strive to do their best every day." Teachers met with parents during a special weekend workshop to discuss how to improve education. Teachers also visited the students' homes, often supplying special reading materials. Parents were encouraged to frequently visit their children in class. The four hundred children who were involved in this program showed a six-month gain in reading achievement more than those children not involved (Riouz 1980).

The Wisconsin Research and Development Center for Cognitive Learning program also involved contracts. Parents promised to participate in twice-weekly reading conferences and to engage in a variety of reading-related activities, including visiting the children's classes, reading cooking recipes with their children, and going to the library with them. The teacher promised to meet twice a week with each child and to prepare a weekly progress report to send home to the parent. In the experiment, the children who had formed a learning partnership with their parents gained twelve months' achievement in reading scores, while a control group of children who did not participate in the experiment progressed only one month ahead (Riouz 1980).

Another local program sought to assist parents in their role as their children's first and most important reading teacher. The program, officially labeled the Preschool Readiness Outreach Program, quickly acquired the acronym PROP—a prop for parents. PROP's primary purpose was to share with parents ideas of ways they could help their three- to five-year-old children develop beginning reading skills. Central to PROP was the belief that every child's life has 1) activities that with a little planning can become beginning or prereading learning experiences; 2) "junk" that with a little work can be transformed into a game to encourage reading; and 3) parents, who with a little prop, can provide their children with experiences to extend beginning and prereading skills. Two formats were used: weekly workshops and monthly pamphlets.

Most parent-child activities in these studies were simple, productive, and inexpensive. The most important elements in each one were regular contact between parents and teacher and communication between parents and child.

Teachers should find little difficulty in enlisting parent support in the education process, particularly concerning reading. Most parents want to help. Not only do they derive immediate satisfaction from their own abilities to communicate, but they also sense rewards as they see their child progress. Any hesitancy they may originally feel at helping the school should be eliminated by the positive effects of their active cooperation and participation. In most cases, active participation significantly enhances parents' esteem for the school and what it is trying to do. They become enthusiastic about enlarging the scope of the parent education programs (DeFranco 1973).

The time is propitious indeed to capitalize on that sense of cooperation when we discuss the teaching of reading. A watchful parent can steer his or her child out of a nonreading cycle and into a level of reasonable skill. Concerned parents can help substantially in teaching the nation's children to read more proficiently.

Adult Education: Parents and Teachers

Adult education plays a major role in expanding parental involvement in a child's learning-to-read process. Thus, as the initial programs become better known, demand for them will undoubtedly increase and existing parent education departments will expand. School districts with no parent education program will no doubt be mandated to create one. Teachers of elementary and secondary classes may find themselves facing an evening class of adults (parents). In fact, professional teachers should assume that they are teachers of parents as well as of children.

Teaching parents how to help their children read appears deceptively simple. Some people may believe that parents will only need to know a few simple steps and to become familiar with the readers or texts used in the school. Unfortunately, such a cursory orientation would probably not only be inadequate, but also would do more harm than good.

Much more is involved in the parent-child relationship and in the interaction that should take place as a child learns to read. Parents need to know both how children grow and learn and how best to teach them. Attitudes, timing, person-to-person communication, and degree of patience are but a few of the relevant topics that need to be discussed. Added to these are techniques to keep the adults motivated, interested, and successful in what they are undertaking. Teachers who are accustomed to teaching children find that the tactics needed for teaching adults are quite different from those used in the elementary or secondary classroom. Nothing turns a parent off more quickly than being treated like a child!

A need exists, then, for both teacher and parent training. According to DeFranco (1973), the former can probably be accomplished in a concentrated inservice program with a minimum of twelve hours (preferably twenty). The course content should include information on characteristics of adult learners, techniques for working with adults, the psychology of parent-child relationships, and methods and materials related to helping children with reading. These subjects can be presented to the teachers through films, role plays, games, and workshops for making appropriate reading accessories. Teachers should also get together for additional periodic refresher meetings to share experiences, discuss problems, and offer support and suggestions for solving problems.

Parental involvement and thus parent training should begin during the child's preschool, kindergarten, and elementary years, since parents' help is most influential and since parents seem most interested in helping their children during those years. This training program needs to give parents some general, common-sense guidelines to help them actively participate on the home-school team. Some of these guidelines include:

• Finding out what role the child's teacher wants them to play in education.
• Making the climate for doing homework pleasant for the child.
• Showing interest in what the child does at school.
• Offering encouragement and guidelines for homework without doing it for the child.
• Encouraging the child's other pursuits and interests.
• Enriching the child's experiences in and out of the home.
• Reading what the child reads and discussing it with him.
• Taking the child to the public library to borrow children's books.
• Reading to the child as much as possible.
• Having the child practice reading aloud.

• Having the child make up stories, poems, riddles, song lyrics, and so forth (DeFranco 1973).

Also, parents need to be sure that children are receiving proper nutrition, enough rest, appropriate clothing, and opportunity in the home for quiet study and play with other children. And parents need to set the example by showing their children that reading is important and enjoyable.

Training courses for parents can be structured in various ways. Type One (twelve to twenty hours of instruction) offers the general principles of how a child learns to read, some background in child psychology as it relates to readiness and motivation, and some suggestions for simple to complex enrichment activities at each level of reading. The course should allow time for making appropriate reading accessories, such as letter, word, phrase, sentence, or picture cards; scrap books of related pictures and words; and simple puppets or flannel board cut-outs for story telling. If the parents practice how to use some of these devices in either role-play or workshop situations, they will have better skills when working with their children.

Type Two (twenty to forty hours of instruction) is an in-depth version of the above. This course includes more specifics on child psychology with greater emphasis on parent-child interaction as it relates to learning. This longer course offers more information as well as more time to apply what has been learned while the parents are still under a teacher's guidance.

Type Three is an ongoing workshop and demonstration combined. Parents observe classroom reading lessons for brief periods, meeting afterward with a teacher to discuss what they have watched. After the discussion, the teacher gives suggestions for suitable home extension and enrichment activities and lets parents practice using reading-readiness techniques in role-play situations.

Type Four, the most time-consuming method of parent education, involves teacher and parent working on a one-to-one basis through private conferences. Teachers should prepare printed material with detailed guidelines for parents in advance. The materials should provide specific information to supplement the conference sessions. The primary advantage of the one-to-one approach is that the teacher can custom design the work to the needs of the individual child and parent.

Type Five is designed for parents of children who read very little if at all and therefore require remedial reading work. Enrollment in these classes should be limited so that everyone has the opportunity to learn by doing—as compared with learning through the printed word. They need to participate in discussions and role-plays and to practice reading games to be used with the children. In this course, emphasis is on the significance of parental patience and optimism in helping the child to progress as compared with the acquisition of large quantities of new information.

Type Six consists of occasional symposia or panel discussions on children's reading. These panels serve primarily as a general orientation without permitting much active audience participation and without teaching many practical or specific strategies. Information given in this way may overwhelm and discourage a parent and make learning for the parent more difficult.

Type Seven courses train parents to lead book discussion clubs for older elementary, junior, and senior high school children. Currently, Junior Great Books discussion groups are gaining in popularity.

In all parent education programs, teachers should provide parents with a body of relevant information they can select from to apply to their own needs. As parents gain experience in deciding what is best for them and their children, their self-confidence as parents grows. Frequently, the growth of self-confidence results in improved parent-child relationships.

The process becomes a cycle: parental interest leads to parent-child interaction, which leads to a higher degree of success for the child in his reading ventures and more child and parental satisfaction. Parents acquire a deeper understanding and empathy for a child during reading tasks and become more patient with the child's idiosyncratic pace and method of learning. The parent gains respect for the child's ability to concentrate and persevere. Thus, parent-child relationships are greatly enhanced through mutually shared experiences, especially if parents and children enjoy what they do together (DeFranco 1973).

Increasing Parent Awareness

In addition to parent training courses, teachers can use the following aids to direct parents in helping their children to read:

● Newspaper columns. Since many parents read the local newspaper, teachers can reach them through a regular monthly or weekly column. The column can be written in a question and answer format, based upon those questions that parents ask most frequently. Teachers should not talk down to parents and should answer questions succinctly.

● Parent Resource Rooms. Some parents stay away from school because they feel intimidated or unwelcome. One way to help parents feel comfortable is to arrange rooms just for them. Empty classrooms can be made into parent resource rooms. Parents can use the rooms for three main purposes: 1) for informal meetings to discuss the reading program with teachers or other school personnel, 2) as workrooms for making learning devices and reading games for use at home, and 3) as libraries for reading materials to help parents teach their children how to read.

• Reading progress letters. The New Haven Public Schools use a basal reading program. To secure parental involvement in this program, the reading staff has prepared a series of take-home stories with comprehension questions for each reading level. These stories, distributed after a child completes a reading level, are accompanied by a letter informing parents that their child has successfully completed a segment of the reading program and should be encouraged to continue progressing by completing the at-home assignments.

• Reading homework program. Parents often complain that the schools do not give homework assignments. Homework assignments, if kept at a reasonable level, promote an ideal opportunity for the parent to interact with the child. In fact, dealing with educational content can provide the chance for a more creative experience. Creative assignments that children do not perceive as drudgery can be stimulating and fun for both parent and child.

• Programs involving children. One of the most effective ways to elicit a large turnout at parent-teacher meetings is to involve children in the program. Schools in New Haven have been encouraged to devote at least one of their meetings to a reading-related program with children. Whether it is choral speaking, a play, or a skit, children perform something that emanates from a reading activity.

• Reading recipes. A set of step-by-step "recipes" are useful to help parents reinforce their children's reading skills. Recently, a committee of parents and teachers in New Haven developed sixty-four reading recipes, using practical ideas written in an easy-to-follow format and printed on small cards. Two recipes are sent home each week and parents use them. One example is "ABC Dusting." Objective: to reinforce alphabetical order. Ingredients: room to be dusted, pencil and paper. Procedure: Help your child make a list of the things in the room that need to be dusted. Tell the child that you would like to dust each object in alphabetical order. Using the list that you have made, ask the child, "What should we dust first?" "Second?" Have the child number each object alphabetically. The first few times, work with the child. Later, give him a list to work on alone.

There are many other practical and effective ways of involving parents in a school reading program. Regardless of the mode or program model, interaction between home and school not only helps parents help their children become better readers, but also lets parents know that the schools are fulfilling a commitment to provide the best possible reading program for their children (Crisculo 1980).

The Important Preschool Years

Ideally, parents need to begin learning about the role they can play in their child's education (particularly learning to read) when the child is of preschool age. Parents who are able to build reading readiness in their children before the start of formal instruction guide their children away from the nonreading syndrome. Experiments have shown that children who get an early start at communicating usually perform better in school.

In courses for the parents of preschoolers, teachers should provide clear and simple guidelines to acquaint parents with the value of audio and visual infant stimulation. Parents should learn the significance of verbal communication as a preparation for learning and some simplified games and materials appropriate for each development stage. Courses also need to present parents with specific suggestions for how to teach fundamental language concepts, such as top and bottom, up and down, first, middle and last, and so forth; and how to help children learn to sort objects according to similarities and differences, comprehend groups and categories, and associate and relate objects and events. Parents also need specific suggestions for stimulating the child to ask questions and search for reasons and answers. They need to know how to interest their children in stories and books, how to make their own books, and how to use words to describe the world as they see it.

Parents of preschoolers will find that getting involved with their child's learning patterns is a fairly easy process. They will be able to see proof of the value of their efforts as their children develop curiosity and awareness of the world. They will discover that the educative process has no real secrets. With encouragement from parent educators, children can learn to understand why certain experiences make learning, and especially learning to read, more meaningful and fun.

Parent-Teaching Methods with Preschool and Elementary Children

Reading to a child is dually beneficial. The child grows emotionally from the affective interaction and progresses intellectually toward reading readiness and academic achievement. Even reading to infants is worthwhile. Parents, however, need to understand how to read to their children to most effectively prepare them for intellectual development.

An experiment by Grunagh and Jester (1972) measured mothers' skills at reading to their children. Results showed great variance in the ways parents shared the book with their children and the effects of their methods. Mothers' methods ranged from rather perfunctory questions and comments to very complete descriptions of each picture and animated reading of the words. An example of each of these methods with the child's response illustrates the importance of proper mother-child interaction.

In the first example, the mother takes the book and turns to the first page with a picture of two stuffed animals and a toaster. She points to the toaster and says to her three-year-old child, "Look at that." The child appears to look where the mother is pointing, but says nothing.

The mother turns the page, points to a trumpet that a stuffed kitten is holding and says, "Look at that. What's that?" The child does not answer, but does look where the mother is pointing.

The mother moves on to the next page and points to a stuffed puppy on the floor. She says to the child, "Look at that." Again, the child seems to be observing, but gives no response, either verbally or physically. The mother continues through the remainder of the book, making one comment per page and acting as though she does not expect the child to respond.

This example does not illustrate the minimum amount of interaction observed. Some mothers simply turn the pages of the book and hold it up to the child saying, "See, see." The child's tendency in this instance is to look at the book passively until the last page is turned.

In the second example, mother and child talk at great length about the book and the pictures. The mother asks questions about the book and follows them up if the child does not reply. She asks the child to relate the picture to his own life by saying such things as, "Look at the mixer. I'll bet they're making a birthday cake. Remember when Mommy made you a birthday cake and how you helped? Do you think the kitten will get to lick the spoon when the mother is done?" Mothers who used this approach usually elicited more response from their children than mothers who used other approaches.

Children need to be active participants in the learning process. They learn best through direct experience with people and materials in their environment. Asking young children to sit for long periods of time for rote, abstract learning is asking for trouble. Young children are capable of and eager to learn many things, but always learn best through active participation. While this mode of learning may not always be convenient for the teacher or the parent, it is the one that will encourage greatest success.

Parents and teachers who give children early experiences with literature and books can increase a child's understanding of many basic cognitive and social concepts. For example, as the parent reads or shares a book, the book can be held so the child can clearly and easily see the picture, interact about or point to the pictures of objects, calling them by name. The easier and more natural this is, the more the child will learn to "enjoy learning." After the shared experience, the child may attempt to retrieve the story by reading it to himself (Strickland 1980).

Some considerations listed below may be helpful in guiding parents to effective, spontaneous interaction that will encourage reading readiness:

• Elaborate excursions, activities, or projects are not necessary to stimulate a child's intellectual development. Daily living is rich with experience opportunities. Cooking, cleaning, making or arranging things, caring for grandparents, family, and friends, and caring for pets are all good examples.

• A child's spontaneous curiosity and exploratory behavior need to be encouraged, not discouraged. Parents should be interested in what their children discover and should ask questions, help collect things, and discuss these situations with them.

• Children should be encouraged to call on adults for information and explanations. They also need to understand, however, that not all adults want to help all the time. Children need to learn that there are times when adults, even those generally willing to answer questions, have other interests or responsibilities demanding attention and will not be helpful.

Basic Strategies

Children need to develop effective communication skills as part of the learning-to-read process. In order to help young children develop communication skills, teachers and parents can play the following games with them:

• Point out an object. How many words can you think of to describe it?

• Choose three things commonly found around the house, two that are alike and one different (for example, two forks and one spoon). How are they alike? What makes them different from each other?

• Print a letter of the alphabet on each page of a notebook. Have your child find words in newspapers and magazines that begin with that letter, cut them out, and paste them on the appropriate page.

• Identify animals in the zoo that begin with respective sounds, such as B-B-B-B = Bear.

• Cut out a magazine or newspaper picture that has many different objects in it. Circle one object. Ask the child, "Can you circle the other things in the picture that begin with the same sound?"

• Make up riddles. "What begins with the sound 'm' and shines at night?" (Riouz 1980).

Parental Involvement and Older Children

Parents of junior and senior high school age children are usually much more complacent about their child's reading abilities. They assume that the child knows how to read and that the motivation to do so will be provided by the school. Frequently, however, these middle years are the time when a child needs the most parental encouragement to continue reading. Again, teacher leadership in adult education programs can take the initiative for providing parents with clear guidelines.

In these courses, teachers should offer suggestions for how to use newspapers, magazines, fiction, poetry, and plays in shared reading at home. They should also help parents analyze, discuss, and evaluate teaching procedures that will work with teenagers. The goal of a home enrichment program for children of this age is to expose the child to the value of reading for pleasure. Often, parental involvement is the key to stimulating the older child to form those reading-for-pleasure habits.

Ways Parents Can Help Children in School

Following are some specifics to guide parents as they help their children learn. These techniques take no formal training—just time. Some suggestions may seem obvious, but most parents do not follow them all. Teachers might consider sending all parents a checklist similar to this one.

1. Keep your children healthy. Should the school nurse or doctor inform you that your child has a health problem, discuss it. He or she can help get the assistance you need. Seeing, hearing, and feeling well are essential to learning.

2. Talk with your children. Talk naturally. Do not use baby talk no matter how young the child. The more words a child can understand and say, the more easily he or she learns to read and understand.

3. Listen to your children. Encourage them to talk about their everyday activities. Make sure you give them the chance to initiate conversation during meals and on other suitable occasions. Your children will learn to express themselves if they know you will give them your attention.

4. Praise your children. Praise and recognition reinforce and encourage learning. Reading, for example, is enjoyable but hard work. Children need your support in order to persist. Praise them when they succeed and help them when they have problems.

5. Be patient with your children. Even though you work with them and help them with their homework, they may make the same mistakes many times. Do not despair. Some experts say that new learning may require more than fifteen repetitions before it is absorbed. Since learning cannot take place in a tense atmosphere, do not become angry or impatient. If you find yourself "losing your cool," stop and do something else for a while.

Parents and teachers must always keep in mind that making mistakes is a natural and necessary part of the learning process. Learning is developmental and is essentially a process of making something new fit into an existing construct of the environment. For example, the child who might understand the concept of orange will possibly call a tangerine an orange. However, with additional experiences and stimulation, the child will accommodate the new information.

6. Avoid comparing your children. Each child is unique. Some children learn faster than others. If your children seem to be moving at a slow rate, do not blame them or worry them about it. You will discover

their untapped reserve of attributes and talents with time. Let them know you love them for what they are and that you will continue to love them no matter how they do in school.

7. Set the stage for good prereading, reading, or homework habits. Try to provide a quiet, well-lighted place with room and proper storage for books, papers, pens, pencils, and other tools related to reading.

8. Schedule home storytime or study on a regular basis. To succeed, many children need a regular study time, free of interruptions and distractions. If your school children are not given a homework assignment, this scheduled time can be used for review, reading for pleasure, or some type of learning activity. If your children are preschoolers, this schedule can establish useful reading-readiness habits. A good idea is to provide each of your children with a notebook so that both of you can keep track of information and assignments. If your child does not know how to write, you can write for him as he tells you his ideas, or he can draw a picture to account for his ideas.

9. Set a bedtime and stick to it. Learning is hard work and requires full use of all faculties. Your children will be in the proper frame of mind and ready for learning only if they report to school each morning well rested.

10. See that your children's school attendance is excellent. When children miss school, they may miss the presentation of new information or the practice with a difficult concept. Once they fall behind their group, they must struggle especially hard to catch up. Some children can never quite adjust after frequent or extended absences from school.

11. Know exactly how your children are doing in school. If you find out that they are having academic or other problems, do not wait to be contacted by the school. Take the initiative by making an appointment to talk the problem over with the teacher. If you cannot get to school, send a note asking the teacher to contact you by telephone. Find out how you can help. Perhaps you can provide information about your children and family that will help school personnel respond with greater understanding to your child's situation.

12. Make family mealtimes nutritional, positive, and meaningful. Mealtime can provide the ideal setting for talking together, sharing events of the day, and discussing individual problems and aspirations. In a relaxed family atmosphere, youngsters have a chance to test their debating skills in friendly arguments and to talk out their differences of opinion. Such discussions will help develop your children's self-confidence and encourage them to speak up in the classroom. Try to keep a regular and all-member-present dinner hour and do not allow the television to interfere with this perfect opportunity for family communication.

13. Make television your servant, not your master. Children learn a lot from television—both good and bad. Help them choose appropriate

programs to watch. Then watch with them and afterwards discuss what you have seen. This approach to television can help your children learn discretion and develop new interests that they can learn more about through reading.

One system for choosing programs carefully is to get the family together once a week to consider the television listings. By choosing carefully in advance, you will help your children consider television only as one of many entertainment or learning tools available, and you will give them a valuable thinking and decision-making experience.

14. Take your children places. Visits to nature and science centers, art museums, train and subway stations, airports, farms, factories, shipyards, supermarkets, pet shops, and so forth will help broaden their experiences. Such diverse activities are vital in readying young children for reading.

15. Read with your children. Rarely is there a child who is not delighted to have a parent or older friend read to them. However, remember to read with your children, not only to them. Not long ago, a young teacher was trying to read a book to a small group of five-year-olds. The children kept interrupting with questions and comments, frequently turning back a page or two and saying such things as, "Let me see the lion again," and "See the mouse with the hat?" Finally, the teacher said in an angry tone, "Do you want me to read this story or not? If so, hush!" That teacher's scolding kept her students quiet, but turned the youngsters into spectators of the reading process, not participants in it. The experience lost its excitement, and the story was no longer personal.

16. Help your children read. If your children are beginning readers, tell them the words they cannot yet read so that they can move along and maintain interest. Later, you can assist them in figuring out the harder words for themselves.

17. Have your children read to you or tell the story by pictures. Encourage them to look at the book or read the story to themselves before they read it to you. This practice will give them confidence and a greater understanding of what they have read or are preparing to read. It will also make the story more interesting to them.

18. Listen as your children tell you about what they have read. Reading is not reading unless it is accompanied by understanding. Therefore, when your child shows understanding by wanting to tell you about what he or she has read, you should be interested.

19. Provide a wide variety of reading materials in your home. Children learn by example rather than by precept. If you have books, magazines, and newspapers readily available and in use, your children will see that reading is a source of pleasure and information. It is infinitely more effective for your children to see you reading often than it is for you to tell them to read.

20. Give your children books as birthday or holiday gifts. Children who have books they can call their very own are motivated to read. The arrival of books mailed directly to your children, with their names on the labels or cartons, provides a strong incentive for reading.

21. Tempt your children with paperbacks. For a number of young readers, there is something formidable about hardcover books. Paperbacks are often much more attractive. Because paperbacks are less costly, you can provide many more and a greater variety of books.

22. Intrigue your children with their own magazine subscriptions. Many youngsters, even those preschoolers or children not keen on the idea of reading at all, might not be able to resist the appeal of receiving their very own magazine. Reluctant readers suddenly find themselves poring over instructions for easy, do-it-yourself projects, riddles, puzzles, and stories. Before they know it, they are "hooked" on reading, anxiously awaiting the next issue of their magazine.

23. Get your children interested in daily newspapers. Read and discuss articles with them (Senger and Patterson 1970).

Summary

The most important thing parents can do to promote the child's readiness in learning to read is to reinforce what the teacher expects as well as to establish an appropriate learning environment. Parents are indeed a source of educational support for children. The practice of home teaching has merit, and parents can strive to provide a household learning environment conducive to their child's education. The following helpful ten–point guide will assist parents in preparing a proper and productive domestic learning atmosphere. These guidelines are also recommended for professionals who help parents avoid alienating themselves from their children.

1. *The learning situation must be positive.* Do not initiate a home-teaching session to punish a child for doing poorly in school.
2. *Working with a child must be enjoyable for the parents.* Parents should not feel compelled to work with the child because of frustration.
3. *A teaching session should be kept short.* Never work with your child after he or she is exhausted.
4. *Whenever possible, require the child to perform activities that can be observed and recorded.* This will assure the exactness of the encounter, which in turn may be recalled and discussed in a parent education setting.
5. *Provide feedback for work well done.* Frequent positive comments, such as "good job," "right on," and "looking good" will encourage the student.
6. *Use a quiet and comfortable work location.* Avoid distractions that will hamper the session.

7. *Sessions should be planned for a time convenient for both you and the child.* Avoid scheduling the work session during a favorite television show, playtime with a friend, other household responsibilities, or any other time set aside for a valued activity.
8. *The learning task should be kept within the ability of the child.* The parents should remember that they are not totally responsible for the child's educational program.
9. *Personalize the learning activity whenever possible.* This evokes a favorable attitude and response from the child.
10. *Present the child with situations in which he or she can apply new knowledge.* This will help the child retain what has been learned.

Parents have the most significant influence on their children during the early developmental years. Especially significant is the influence parents have in helping their children learn to read. Thus, teachers and parent educators need to encourage and equip parents with specific methods for supporting children in this learning process.

References

Cooke, P. and Appolloni, T. 1975. Parental involvement in the schools: Ten postulates of justification. *Education* 96:168–69.

Crisculo, N. 1979. Activities that help involve parents in reading. *The Reading Teacher* 32:417–19.

DeFranco, E. B. 1973. Parent education: Reading. *Adult Leadership* 21:319–23, 346.

Howard, N. K. 1972. Mother child home learning programs: An abstract bibliography. *ERIC*. Urbana, Ill.: University of Illinois.

Larrick, N. 1976. From "hands off"—to "parents we need you." *Childhood Education* 52:134–37.

Rich, D. 1976. The family as educators: A letter to principals. *National Elementary Principals* 55:71–77.

Riouz, W. 1976. *You can improve your child's school.* New York: Simon and Schuster.

Schaefer, E. S. 1972. Parents as educators: Evidence from cross-sectional, longitudinal, and intervention research. *Young Children* 27:227.

Senger, L. and Patterson, C. 1970. *Ways to help babies grow and learn: activities for infant education.* Denver: World Press, Inc.

Spadefore, G. 1979. A guide for the parent as tutor. *The Exceptional Parent* 9:E17–18.

Strickland, D. 1980. Take part in a miracle. Help your child learn to read. *Early Years* 11:5–9.

Vukelich, C. 1978. Parents and teachers: A beginning reading program. *The Reading Teacher* 31:524–28.

Home Involvement Using the Yawkey Parent-Child Play Model

Thomas D. Yawkey

Thomas D. Yawkey is an associate professor in early childhood education at Pennsylvania State University. He has authored, coauthored, and edited more than 100 articles and books, including Learning Is Child's Play *and* The Self-Concept of the Young Child, *both published by Brigham Young University Press. Dr. Yawkey's primary research interest is in child's play.*

A few of the important questions early childhood educators and home visitors must ask about parent-home involvement programs include "What procedures can home visitors use to work with parents in the home?" "What are some of the things parents need to know to work with their children at home?" and "How do home visitors develop a model with parents for parent-child involvement that is systematic, effective, and efficient, yet flexible?" The purpose of this narrative is to approach some of these questions by discussing the following:

- the importance of parents working with their children at home
- ways to implement the Yawkey Parent-Child Play model
- parent-child play strategies and activities in the model
- the results of using the model.

Importance of Parental Involvement

The results of studies on how the youngster's formative years affect present and future growth, how family and home involvement programs

118

affect a child's development and learning, and the recognition of play as a natural medium for parent-child interaction have brought about some of the educational reform of the present and past two decades. These factors also point out the importance of showing parents how to work with their children in play activities.

The Formative Years

The formative years (birth through eight years of age) are the most important ones since a major portion of the youngster's potential for intellectual and attitudinal growth develops within this timespan. The very young child conceptualizes by physically involving himself in his world, by doing. However, the older child learns to think about his physical actions without first doing them. This conceptual ability affects several important mental concepts that develop during the formative years—transformation, reversibility, and decentration—that later become keys to growth and learning. *Transformation* is the ability to conceptualize the beginning and ending points of an event and make the transition between these points by connecting interrelated, smaller events in order. For example, the child realizes that in order to get from his house to grandma's, he and mother must drive or walk over hills and cross a bridge. His house is the beginning point, grandma's house is the ending point, and the driving or walking over hills and crossing the bridge are all related events that make the transition. Understanding *reversibility* lets the youngster conceptualize, reason through a set of steps, arrive at a solution, then mentally trace his logic from the solution back through the set of steps. He can think about getting from his house to grandma's, then can reverse his thinking and return from grandma's house to his. Finally, *decentration* is the ability to focus on the social or physical factors that are important in solving a particular problem rather than on superficial or irrelevant characteristics. For example, while trying to determine which one of two groups has the greater number of objects in it, the child must understand that the number of objects is what is important, not the space they take up.

Since the routines and interactions of the family in the home shape the youngster's cognitive and attitudinal growth, the development of these concepts is directly related to family and parental involvement. Training that focuses on showing parents how to work with their children equips them to act as teachers, socializing agents, and decision makers. It then helps them develop patterns of interaction to use during their child's formative years that promote the development of these important learning skills.

Family and Home Involvement Programs

Educational reforms of the latter sixties, seventies, and now the eighties also emphasize the contributions that family and home involvement programs can make to individual and group learning and development. These contributions develop out of two separate, but interrelated, areas of research (Yawkey and Prewitt-Diaz 1981): the effect both parent and child have on family interactions (Bronfenbrenner 1975, Caldwell 1967, White 1975), and the effect that systematically educating parents in the home has on the child (Gordon 1972; Madden, Levenstein, and Levenstein 1976; Schaefer 1972).

Results from the first area of research highlight the significance of both quantitative and qualitative interactions on development and learning. Within the social and physical setting of the family, interactions take place between the youngster and parent as well as between the parent and youngster. Also, the parent mediates between the youngster and his outside world by exposing the youngster to, and protecting him from, experiences. As a result, the parents act as a type of filter and pass on "the benefits and limitations of their own personalities, conflicts, and cognitive and emotional resources" (Bee et al. 1975, p. 297). As the interactions between parent and child are strengthened, intellectual and emotional elements reinforce each other, building strong emotional attachments between parent and child. These increase the youngster's motivation to pay attention to and learn from the parent (Bronfenbrenner 1975). These relationships within the family are very powerful, effective, and long-lasting; they mold the youngster's present and future learning (Bronfenbrenner 1975). White (1975, p. 4) believes that they have "more of an impact on a child's total . . . development than the formal educational system." Establishing and strengthening these interactions by working with the parents can help shape the child's development, feelings, aspirations, and attitudes.

The second area of research explores the effect of educating parents at home in order to maximize their potential as the child's first and most influential teachers. It emphasizes the importance of training parents to work with their children, acting as teachers, decision makers, and socializing agents (Schaefer 1972) in their child's development. This helps the child in a number of ways. First, studies show impressive and sustained intellectual gains of from three to five years in young children after the home involvement programs terminate (Donachy 1976, Levenstein 1977, Stevens and King 1978). Children whose parents are trained to work with them at home scored significantly higher on intelligence tests than children whose parents were not trained. Second, in the Levenstein Mother-Child Home Program, the children involved also scored significantly higher on positive child behavior traits than others not in this program. Third, home involvement programs train parents to more effectively control the environment and events which impinge on the child and to control the reward system by responding to youngsters in positive, negative, or natural ways (Gray 1971). As a result, they can adjust their roles with children, enriching their child-rearing repertoires (Bronfenbrenner 1975, Yawkey 1981). Fourth, as a result of these home involvement programs, parents and children develop more positive attitudes toward themselves and society than those not involved in similar programs (Radin 1972, Yawkey and Prewitt-Diaz 1981). Fifth, target children taught by their parents in home involvement programs influenced and taught the other youngsters in the family, a type of "vertical diffusion" that brought additional positive effects. Obviously the effects of training parents to work with their children at home has a number of advantages, provided that a natural medium for interaction can be used.

Play and Development

A final aspect of the education reforms was the recognition of the significance of child's play. Bruner (1972) and Piaget (1962), for example, feel that play is important because it encourages novel actions. Research studies by Saltz, Dixon, and Johnson (1977), Smilansky (1968), and Yawkey (1981a) show that play benefits the child's development by decreasing his response time while solving tasks; increasing his mean scores on language intelligence tests, orally generated sentences, story interpretation, memory, and empathy; and by mentally preparing him for reading and mathematics. In addition, the power of pretend reaches its maximum potential during the ages two through six (Piaget 1962), within the important formative years. Yet play is an entirely natural activity. From the child's perspective play is pleasant and desirable. The pretend world, imaginary playmates, toys, games, and activities are all fun. Parents are familiar with the types and kinds of toys they buy and typically see playing as a pleasant way their youngsters spend the time at home. All this makes play an ideal medium for parents to use. An additional value of using playtime to enrich a child's learning is that parents can easily be trained to use interactive play strategies through home involvement programs (Yawkey and Prewitt-Diaz 1981).

Based on these major ideas, the Yawkey Parent-Child Play model (PCP) was developed, implemented, and tested.

The Yawkey PCP Model

In using any home involvement model, early childhood teachers and administrators need to thoroughly examine the target parents and children who will be involved, the geographic area in which it will be used, its procedures and teaching materials, and what methods will be used to assess its validity and results. These factors are described and applied to a particular situation in the following section. After examining how this model was used in this particular instance, the early childhood teacher, administrator, and parent may wish to adjust and modify it to better fit their particular situations (Yawkey and Silvern 1977).

Target Parents and Children

The Yawkey PCP model for home involvement was originally developed to use with parents and children from poverty and low-income populations. The United States' guidelines for 1980–81 that define "at or below poverty level" were used as one of two criteria to enroll parents in the project. The second criterion used requested parents to have at least one child enrolled in the local county Head Start.

The PCP project and its importance were explained to interested parents at regional meetings of a Community Action Agency throughout the country; then parents were invited to join either the experimental or control group in the project. After applying the eligibility criteria, twelve of the volunteer families were placed in the experimental groups—those who would be trained to work with their children at home, and twelve were placed in the control group who would not be trained. The parents were white, black, and hispanic; the majority of them were legally defined as single-parent families, and were unemployed and on welfare. Except for one male parent in the experimental group, all the parents were female. They all lived in a fifty-mile radius of an Appalachian city in Central Pennsylvania's coal and mining region, either in and around the city and towns or in geographically isolated or rural areas. During the project, four parents in the control group and four in the experimental group withdrew. This one-third rate attrition occurred because some of the parents found part or full-time employment, one parent removed her child from Head Start, and one decided she no longer wanted to participate.

The sixteen children (eight boys and eight girls) of the project parents were all between the ages of three and five, and had anywhere from zero to four siblings with an average 2½ brothers and sisters apiece.

Once the experimental and control groups were established, all of the parents and children were tested in order to determine if the groups were similar enough to compare validly those who used the model and those who did not.° Pretesting indicated no significant differences. The Yawkey PCP model of home involvement began in December with this pretesting and finished five months later in April with complete posttesting.

Procedure

The parents in the experimental group were given weekly training by home visitors during the five months. The three home visitors were female, in their middle to late twenties, had previous experience working with groups of preschoolers who had special needs, and were paid for

---

°A complete discussion of the tests and their results occurs later in the chapter.

their services. Prior to beginning the project, each home visitor went through a three-hour training session; this explained the behavioral objectives of the project and its intended outcomes, constructive ways of working with project parents, the Yawkey model, and evaluation methods. In addition, before working with the parents on each week's lesson, home visitors received three and one-half hours of training, which included explaining and discussing the lesson's objectives and procedures, demonstrations on how to effectively teach the play strategies, and talking over any problems that had occurred or might occur with particular parents. Anecdotal notes on the parents' performances written down by the home visitor after each session and the results of parental surveys were also discussed, along with any miscellaneous items and questions.

In the weekly meetings with the parents, the home visitors used an instructional model—an established teaching format that identifies the areas to be covered and the time required for each one (Yawkey and Silvern 1977). The instructional model used was structured as follows: parent summarizes and reports from the previous week—five minutes, home visitor explains the current session's objective—ten minutes, home visitor describes the new play routines for the home—fifteen minutes, parent rehearses the play routine—fifteen minutes, home visitor extends the play routine to setting outside the home—ten minutes.

Instructional Model

In summarizing the previous week, the parent reviews last week's play routine and describes how she used it with her child both in and outside the home. This gives the home visitor a chance to see if the parent understands its importance, used it, and used it correctly. As the home visitor listens to this review, she should correct any errors and misunderstandings in a sensitive, constructive way.

After this brief report the home visitor should explain the objectives of the present session, using simple, clear language and concrete examples from common home situations. Each session has from one to three objectives written in behavioral terms that focus on the child's school-related abilities. For example, "When you use this play routine, your child will be able to point to four objects that are blue, orange, brown, and gray and name their colors in less than ten minutes." These objectives help the parents see that by using the play routine their child will learn specific, observable actions that will later help in school, reassuring the parent that she is making a real contribution to her child's growth.

The home visitor then describes and models the new play routine* for the parent, actually showing her what and how to do and say it. Modeling is the most effective way to help the parent clearly understand exactly how to use the new play routine with her child.

---

*Examples of play routines are included later.

In role-playing and rehearsing the play routine, the parent plays back what she observed, showing the home visitor how she will use it with her child at home. This playback gives the home visitor a chance to see how well the parent understands the play routine and to carefully correct the parent's statements and movements. If handled sensitively and honestly, the parent will see this correction as a way to improve her work with her child rather than as criticism.

In extending this new play routine, the home visitor shows the parent how it can be easily used with the child outside the home. With each training session the home visitor should try to choose one different setting outside the home in which the routine is to be used that week. This could include driving in the car, going to the supermarket, visiting a relative's house, or just walking down the street. At the completion of each session, if several minutes of instruction time remain, the home visitor can show the parent an activity to do with the child.

Using this instructional model, the home visitor and parent spend approximately fifty-five minutes per week together. After they finish working with their assigned parents, each home visitor spends about thirty minutes giving oral and objective summaries of the parents' performances during the lesson, listing the play routines used by the parents during the previous week, and writing out postcards that briefly describe one important highlight of that lesson. The visitor then urges the parents to try the new play routine, and reminds them of the next appointment. The home visitors are rotated among the parents to ensure that the parent's performance results from training, not from a particular visitor's actions. Consequently, a home visitor never works with the same parent two consecutive weeks.

Teaching Materials

There are six different types of teaching materials used in the Yawkey PCP model: familiar toys, games, and concrete activities used as part of the play routines; 250-to-300-word children's stories used in the play routines; play and game activities for children in home settings; Memo to Mom/Ditto to Dad—a one-page reminder for the parents; surveys, questionnaires and interviews used by the home visitor to gather information for future lessons; and recollections of actions and comments made by the parents during the home visits. The home visitor uses the first three teaching materials while training the parent, who will then use them with her child. The other three teaching materials are used only with the parents or as a resource for the home visitor.

The first teaching material the home educator uses is the child's favorite toys, games, and activities. With these materials the home visitor demonstrates for the parent what to say and do with his child. The parent then practices the play routines on the home visitor, using these toys. In deciding what toys and activities to use, the parent needs to choose only those the child knows and likes. Examples of familiar toys, games, and concrete activitives that might be used include dolls, Old Maid, trucks, watching favorite TV cartoon characters, playing house, and walking to grandma's house. Also, since using familiar toys, activities, and games in the play routines produces greater development and learning in preschoolers than using unfamiliar ones (Ellis 1973, Yawkey and Prewitt-Diaz 1981), new toys and games should not be used until the child has time to play with them in any way he wants to and to figure out what they do and how they function.

The second teaching material used is the children's story. Children's stories can be summarized by the home visitor onto a double-spaced, typewritten page and should contain a maximum of 250 to 300 words. They can be taken directly from one of the child's books, retaining familiar words, phrases, and sentences for easy comprehension. The children's stories chosen for use in this project typically were action stories with domestic, heroic, and adventure themes that appealed to preschoolers; had main characters with whom children could easily identify; depicted all races, languages, cultures, and gender positively; and had settings similar to where the children lived (Yawkey and Yawkey 1976).

Usable stories can also be found in the public and school libraries. *Mr. Strong* is one good example. The male character in this delightful story uses his great physical powers to perform heroic feats, eats rather peculiar food, and lives in a rural area. If necessary the home visitor can make up a children's story that fits the requirements and distribute it to the parents to use. *Sandy's Surprise*, a story written by a home visitor, centers on the adventures of a family pet growing up in a rural family.

With these selected stories, the home visitor shows the parent how to use a story in a play routine. After observing the demonstration, the parent practices reading the story and using it in the play routine. If some parents are unable to read, the home visitor can ask them to make up their own stories. For example, they can tell short histories about their parents, experiences they had as a child, or highlights of interesting or amusing episodes about family members. These homemade stories are ideal material for play routines.

The third teaching material home visitors use is play and game activities that parents can do with their youngster either at home or outside the home. These activities are simple, require only small amounts of time and concrete objects, and can be used almost anywhere the parent and child go together. At the end of each weekly training session, the home visitor explains the next activity to the parent; this means that the parent has only one new activity to learn and practice each week. The purpose of these activities is to increase the quality and quantity of time the child and parent interact with one another. One example of an activity used in this play model is Twenty Questions.

For this game, the parent asks the child to help put some grocer-ies away. The parent asks the child to manipulate the cans, boxes, and envelopes, and the parent asks questions about each item the child handles. The child learns such concepts as large, small, above, below, shapes, colors, and categorization of objects in the cupboard (Yawkey and Prewitt-Diaz 1981, p. 9).

Other activities include concentration, floor games, or scavenger hunts.

The fourth type of teaching material used is the Memo to Mom/Ditto to Dad, a one-page, typed handout left with the parent at the end of each session. This reminder describes the play routine the parent learned and suggests how to use it both inside and outside the home. Following is a sample reminder.

Memo to Mom/Ditto to Dad

A Reminder: Session Number _____

1. The play strategy or routine for this session.
   a. Read or tell a story to your child while he listens.
   b. Praise him as he listens.
2. Try this play strategy or routine *in the home* with:
   a. the stories you read or tell your child (for example, try the story *Sandy's Surprise*).
   b. the stories using the youngster's favorite TV or cartoon characters.
3. Try this play strategy or routine *outside the home*: this week do an activity with your child in the yard, the park, or a recreation area.

The fifth kind of material used asks the parent for information about the child and family to use as a basis for planning future lessons with the parent. The home visitor gathers the information at the end of each session through homemade or commercial surveys and questionnaires and through informal interviews with the parents. Some examples of useful information are favorite toys or household objects the child likes to play with, how he plays with these toys, television shows the child watches, and how many hours during the week the child spends watch-ing TV. This material is valuable resource information to help fit the play routines into the specific activities, situations, and objects common to the family.

The final teaching material is the recollection of comments made by parents. At the end of each visit, the home visitor writes down anecdot-al recordings on 8½-by-11 inch lined paper. These recollections can provide further insight into ways of working with the parent and solving problems that might hinder constructive home visitor-parent-child dia-logues. Recollections can also help identify the strengths and weaknesses of that particular lesson. In order for them to be helpful they should clearly identify the parent's actions or comments.

1. Mrs. Garcia° attended to my demonstration for two minutes and correctly practiced the play routine.
2. Mrs. White said, "I didn't have time to use the play idea with my child this past week."
3. Mrs. Black said that her girl likes to play largely with puzzles, footballs, legos, and plastic spoons.
4. Mrs. Anne said, "I didn't watch my child play, but I did talk with her about her watching Space Ghost—her favorite TV cartoon."

Recollections focusing on lesson strengths and weaknesses might include something like the following:

1. The reminder handouts strengthened Mrs. Black's understanding and use of the play strategy in this session.
2. More specific examples of Charlie's toys were needed to improve the lesson.

All of these teaching materials have the advantage of being simple to use in a training session. The favorite toys, the short stories, and the activities and games are then used directly by the parent while working with her child in the play routines.

Play Routines

The play routines are all action-oriented, highly structured descriptions of what parents do and say to children; they also identify the child's growth that will result from using the routine. In the Yawkey play model, the home visitor introduced a new play routine to the parents each week. These were referred to as *plans* or *ideas*, terms that are less academic and more readily used by the parents than *play routines*. The model uses a number of basic routines; six have been chosen for examples here. Each of these plays contains a specific set of related actions that the parent is asked to do with her child in a play session. These also indirectly suggest what the youngster will say and do. Since these actions are sequential, during the training session the home visitor emphasizes that the parent must follow the order. Each of the plans and their actions can be repeated over and over again, depending on the child's attention, his desire to keep playing, and his need for continued parent-child interaction.

Plan 1. Join in and help your child play by prompting him as he plays, praising his pretend and imitative actions and activities with approval or affection.

Plan 2. Join in and help your child play by talking to him as he plays, praising his actions and statements after he responds to you, adding objects to his play activities that are related to what he is doing, then

---

° All names are fictitious.

praising his actions and statements after he responds to the addition of the objects.

Plan 3. Join in and help your child play by talking to him as he plays, praising his actions and statements after he responds to you, adding objects that are not related to what he is doing, then praising his actions and statements after he responds to the addition of the unrelated objects.

Plan 4. Join in and help your child play by reading or telling a favorite story, asking him to retell the story so others can understand it, praising his retelling of each part of the story, and extending his oral description of the story while he retells it.

Plan 5. Join in and help your child play by reading or telling a story while he listens to it, asking him to act out the story so others will understand it, praising his acting of each part, and extending his description of the story by modeling and expanding on his movements after he acts the story out.

Plan 6. Join in and help your child play by having him select his favorite toy or game or play activity, making up a simple story for him that contains this choice, and then asking questions related to the story to help him use this object to answer correctly, praising him after he responds.

A thorough discussion of each plan follows.

Plan 1. The home visitor asks the parent to observe the child's play and then joins in by first prompting him with open-ended comments or questions consistent with his play. For example, suppose a child is playing house with a doll. As the youngster rocks the doll, the parent might prompt by saying "Does Dolly feel sleepy?" "Why?" "It will soon be time for Dolly to go to school. Show her getting up and dressing herself," or "How would Dolly feel if she is hungry and wants to eat?"

The home visitor instructs the parent to then wait for the child to respond. This "wait time" is valuable for it gives the youngster time to think about answering and gives the parents a moment to decide how to respond. After the child responds to the adult's ideas verbally or with his actions, the parent is to praise him. This praise shows the parent's approval. Low-income parents may often feel that praising and showing approval for what the child says or does correctly is not necessary because "they know when they do things that are right or wrong" (Yawkey and Prewitt-Diaz 1981). Or the parents may feel that rewarding a child when he is right may spoil him, lead to disobedience and "bigger things," or similar types of child-development old wives' tales (Yawkey and Prewitt-Diaz 1981). Therefore, it is important for the parent to understand that individuals learn better with rewards; the faster the reward is given after a response, the quicker the child learns. With low-income parents especially, the home visitor may need to explain the importance of reward a number of times, asking them to try rewarding and showing approval.

There are two types of reward or approval statements: token or social. Token rewards are concrete things; for example, "For answering me, here is a toy truck for you to play with" or "For saying/doing this, you can visit either the zoo or the circus. Which one would you like to see?" Other token rewards include giving the child special foods to eat, money to spend, and favorite or desired objects. However, the use of social rewards is far more common. This reward includes praise: "Good job for saying/doing this"; "You really know how to do this"; a hug or touching the child affectionately.

After rewarding the child, the parent can prompt again with another play suggestion and again reward his response, continuing this cycle until the youngster begins to tire, lose attention, or does not want to play any longer.

Plan 2. In this plan, the first, second, and fourth actions the parents do are the same as actions learned in Plan 1: prompting and praising. Since each play routine or plan builds on the previous ones, the home visitor actually teaches the parent only a few new actions each week. In plan two only the third action is new. This requires the parent to add objects to the play activities that are thematically related to the activities. The home visitor must first teach the parents to watch the child's play to get an idea of the activity, usually by observing what youngsters do and say in their play roles (Curry and Arnaud 1974). After observing, if the parent is still unsure of what the child is doing, he can simply ask the child to label his play. This procedure is actually faster, easier to use, and more efficient and effective (Yawkey 1981b).

After the play's theme is identified, the parent finds play objects that fit with it and gives them to the child along with a question to help him use them in his play. For example, if the youngster tells the parent he is playing house, the parent may find a toy saucepan and give it to the child, saying, "Show how you could use the saucepan to play house" or "Do you think Dolly would like to eat something you cook for her with this saucepan?" After this comment the parent again gives the youngster some time to think about possible reactions. When the child responds, the parent praises the child's statements and actions. As in plan one, the parent can continue and extend parts three and four by giving the child another object and praising his reactions, repeating this as long as the child is willing to play.

Plan 3. In this plan the first, second, and fourth actions are the same as those in plans one and two. The one different action is adding objects to the child's play that are not related thematically to his play. Using the techniques learned in plan two to identify the theme, such as playing house, the parent finds a toy or an object—a paper clip, a pebble, a block of wood—that is not logically related to this theme. Following the same procedures in plan three the parent hands the unrelated object to the child, cuing its possible use in the play by what he says. "How could you use this paper clip to play house?" "What might mother (whom the child is playing) do with this block of wood?" "Mother looks so hungry. Do you think she might like to eat this pebble? Show what she might do with it." The parent again waits, then praises the child.

An interesting variation of working with unrelated objects can be played with more developmentally advanced and gifted children, using their imagination to turn related objects into unrelated ones and into the play theme. The parent might comment, "Pretend that this spoon (a related object) is a zebra (an unrelated one) and use it in playing house." The child must use his imagination, convert the image of a spoon into a zebra, and figure out a way to fit the zebra into his play.

Plan 4. The use of praise in this plan is the same as the previous ones, but the other three actions are new. The first action in this plan asks the parent to read or tell a favorite story to the child. The parent is taught to introduce the story idea by saying something like "I will read (or tell) you a story, *Mr. Strong.* Listen carefully to find out what he does in the story (or eats or says)." After completing the story, the parent asks the youngster to retell it, praising him as he does. The fourth action the parent uses extends selected sentences of the child's description of the story while he is retelling it. For example, the child may say, "Mr. Strong walks along the road." The parent rewards his statement, then decides whether to use this sentence for extension or to continue with the child's retelling. If the parent decides to extend it, he enlarges and expands this description to make it more real and alive. In extending the sentence, "Mr. Strong walks along the road," the parent might say, "Mr. Strong walks quickly down the dusty road" or "Mr. Strong walks quickly down the dusty road lined with lemon trees," depending on the child's developmental level of thinking and use of language. For the advanced child, the extension might be, "Mr. Strong, with a worried look and a hurried gait, walks quickly down the dusty road lined with lemon trees and disappears over the old, creaky wooden bridge." As the youngster gets the idea of adding description to make the story come alive, the parent again praises him.

Plan 5. In this plan, the first and third actions are used as in previous plans. In the new second action, the parent encourages the child to act out the familiar story after hearing it. Here the child is guided to show and tell what happened in the story, using body movements, physical actions, and words. This combination of body movements, physical actions, and words facilitates intellectual and language growth of preschoolers (Yawkey 1981b). After prompting him to act out the story and praising him for his efforts, instead of extending language, the parent extends the child's physical movements by retelling parts of the story with accompanying movements, adding additional movements for greater description and more detail. This extends the child's actions, providing him with solid examples to use another time. As always, praise and approval are used to ensure sound learning.

Plan 6. While this plan uses praise, its first, second, and third actions are new. First the parent guides the child to select one of his favorite familiar toys. If the child has a hard time choosing, the parent may decide which two play objects the child uses the most, then have him choose one of them, thus helping the child develop and practice decision making and problem solving.

The parent then makes a simple story for the child that has this play object in it. For instance, perhaps the youngster selects a doll. Accordingly, the parent develops a simple short story about this favorite object. "Dolly is so happy today, she's smiling!" or "Dolly says there is no more food in the cupboard and wants to go grocery shopping today!" or "Dolly really wants to wear her pretty green polka-dot dress and dark green shoes when she goes to Aunt Mary's and Uncle Harry's house." The number of words used in ths story, its complexity, and other characteristics will vary, depending on the child's level of intellectual and language growth.

After composing the story, the parent questions the child about the story and presents the youngster with a simple problem to solve. "I really wonder why Dolly is smiling. Do you know why?" "Where will Dolly go to buy her food and what kinds of food will she buy?" or "Why do you suppose Dolly wants to wear her pretty green polka-dot dress and dark green shoes to Aunt Mary's and Uncle Harry's house? I wonder if she will take her purse along when she visits them." In order to solve the question, the youngster has to think about the situation presented in the story and anticipate possible alternatives and solutions. As he does, the parent praises his response.

Each of these six plans can be used over and over. The parent may decide to use a plan again without varying the content and materials, or he may use some variation the next time. In addition, these play routines can be used outside the home—driving in the car, going shopping at the mall, buying food at the supermarket, visiting a friend's house, and in any other settings, events, and activities that parents and children both are involved in.

Testing

In order to evaluate the results of this home involvement model, the parents and children in both the experimental and the control groups were given pretests and posttests. The parents took four tests: the Alpern-Boll test (ABTE), the Parent-Child Play Preference Inventory (PCCP), the Parent-Child Perspective Taking: Parent Scale (PCPC), and the PAAT Inventory: Adult Form (PAAF).

The ABTE is a normed instrument to assess the parent's perceptions of the child's growth in the specific developmental areas: social, physical, communication, self-help, academic, and I.Q. In each of these areas the parents are asked whether or not their child shows a particular behavior or action. If the parent answers yes to the question, the child is scored as showing the behavior and passes the item. When a parent responds no to the question, the child is scored as not showing the behavior and fails the item. All the passes within each area are added together to produce an age score in months for that area. There is also an overall total score that includes all the areas.

The PCCP contains thirty stimulus items presented in a Likert scale format. Parents react to each item on a scale of zero to four points, depending upon how they interpret the item's relevance to them. For example, the PCPP determines the strength of the parents' views on how useful child's play is in developing concepts and skills.

The PCPC contains fifty items, is normed, and also uses a Likert format, this time with a scale ranging from zero through five. It assesses the parent's ability to take the child's role in certain situations at home and at school.

The PAAT is a thirteen-item normed test with a Likert range from one to four. It indicates the parents' feelings for and attitudes about their child in various behavioral settings. All four tests are used in Head Start, private and public kindergartens, and primary grade programs.

Three tests were used in determining how well the child learned under the parents who used the model: the Columbia Mental Maturity Scale (CMMS), the Parent-Child Perspective Taking: Child Scale (PCCS), and the PAAT Inventory: Child Form (PACF).

The CMMS estimates the general reasoning of children in the 3½ to 9 years age range. While it contains a total of ninety-two pictures and figures on cards with accompanying questions, a smaller number of cards and questions are given to each child, depending on his age level. The child points to the one of four or five pictures on each card that he feels correctly answers the questions he is asked. The answer is scored correct or incorrect, totaled for a raw score, then converted to age deviation and percentile rank scores.

The PCCS contains twenty stimulus items used in the Likert scale of one through three to assess the child's ideas about play and the strength of his imaginative play behavior. For example, each item is read the youngster and he indicates how often he does this type of play by saying "Never," "Sometimes," or "Always." Points for each kind of answer are added together for a total score.

The PACF, a twenty-question test, is a normed instrument that assesses the child's ability to take the role of another in certain home and school situations. He is asked to see himself as he feels his mother or father sees him. The child is read the questions and asked to indicate how he feels in these situations by pointing to a happy, sad, or neutral face. The correct answers to the questions are differentially weighted and the points per item are added together to give a total for each type of response.

Four analyses using one-way analysis of variance (ANOVA) designs as described in Myers (1979) were run separately on each of the four pre-tests that the parents took. These tests showed no significant differences between experimental and control-group parents. A similar analysis of the children's test results also indicated no significant difference between the groups or their performance levels. This pretesting showed that the groups could be compared for teaching results.

Results

To test the effects of the Yawkey model on selected parental and child behaviors, two major questions were asked:

Are there any differences between parents enrolled in the Yawkey home-involvement program and those not enrolled in their perceptions of their children's physical, social, communication, self-help, academic, and I.Q. growth, using the ABTE measure; on their views of the usefulness of play for their youngster's learning, using the PCCP test; on their ability to take the role of the youngster in certain situations, using the PCPC measure; and on their attitudes for and feelings about their youngster on the PAAF test?

Are there any differences between children whose parents followed the Yawkey play model and those children whose parents did not in their general reasoning, using the CMMS test, the number of times they perform particular play actions according to the PCCS instrument, and feeling happy or sad in the types of situations tested in the PACF?

In order to answer the first question concerning the parents, four ANOVAS, each consisting of two pre- versus posttests and two experiment versus control group, were run on each of their tests. The ABTE tests results indicate that the parents using the model had significantly higher scores on their perceptions of their children's social, academic, and communication growth than the control group of parents did, although they did not differ significantly on their perceptions of their children's physical, self-help, and I.Q. growth. The PCCP results showed that the parents in the experimental groups had significantly higher scores than the control group in their views about the utility and importance of child's play for development and learning. The PCPC test results indicated that these parents also had greater ability to take their child's role in specific home and school situations; and on the PAAF measure these parents scored significantly higher on positive feelings and attitudes toward their children at posttest times. Outside these results, none of the tests showed any other significant interactional effects.

With the children, three ANOVAs, each consisting of two pre- versus posttests and two experimental versus control group, were run on each test. CMMS results showed significant main and interactional effects. Children who had been involved in the play model scored significantly higher on general reasoning abilities than those in the control group. They also received higher scores on general reasoning in the posttest. The PCCS's significant effects showed that the experimental group of children played more frequently and longer than the control group, particularly at posttest time. However, the PACF test showed that the children did not differ in their ability to take their parent's role in specific home and school situations.

Summary

These results indicate that this particular home-involvement model has potential for use with both parents and children. Early childhood educators who are evolving home-involvement programs to maximize the formative years could use the Yawkey Parent-Child Play model as a basis for training parents to teach at home. At the least, it indicates a type of structure for a home-involvement program.

Bibliography

Bee, H. L.; Van Egeren, L. F.; Streissguth, A. P.; Nyman, A. P.; and Leckie, M. S. 1975. In *Influences on human development*, eds. U. Bronfenbrenner and M. A. Mahoney, pp. 110–31. Hinsdale, Illinois: Dryden.

Bronfenbrenner, U. 1975. Is early intervention effective? In *Influences on human development*, eds. U. Bronfenbrenner and M. A. Mahoney, pp. 47–89. Hinsdale, Illinois: Dryden.

Bruner, J. 1972: The nature and function of immaturity. *American Psychologist.* 43: 1–7.

Caldwell, B. M. 1967. What is the optimal learning environment for the young child? *American Journal of Orthopsychiatry* 37: 8–21.

Curry, N. E., and Arnaud, S. H. 1974. Cognitive implications in children's spontaneous role play. *Theory into Practice.* 13: 273–77.

Day, M., and Parker, R. eds. 1978. *Preschool in action.* Boston: Allyn and Bacon.

Donachy, W. 1975. Parent participation in preschool education. *British Journal of Educational Psychology* 46:31–39.

Ellis, M. J. 1973. *Why people play.* Englewood Cliffs, New Jersey: Prentice-Hall.

Gordon, I. J. 1972. What do we know about parents as teachers? *Theory into Practice* 1:147–49.

Gray, S. W. 1971. The child's first teacher. *Childhood Education.* 48:127–29.

Levenstein, P. 1977. The mother-child home program. In *The preschool in action: exploring early childhood programs.* 2nd ed., eds. M. C. Day and R. K. Parker, pp. 42–63. Boston: Allyn and Bacon.

Madden, J.; Levenstein, P.; and Levenstein, S. 1976. Longitudinal IQ outcomes of the mother-child program. *Child Development.* 47:1015–25.

Myers, J. 1979. *Fundamentals of experimental design.* Boston: Allyn and Bacon.

Piaget, J. 1962. *Plays, dreams and imitation in childhood.* New York: W. W. Norton.

Radin, N. 1972. Three degrees of maternal involvement in a preschool program: impact on mother and child. *Child Development* 43:1355–64.

Saltz, E.; Dixon, D.; and Johnson, D. 1977. Training disadvantaged preschoolers on various fantasy activities: effects of cognitive functioning and impulse control. *Child Development* 48:367–80.

Schaefer, E. S. 1972. Parents as educators: Evidence from cross-sectional longitudinal and intervention research. In *The young child: review of research.* vol. 2, ed. W. W. Hart, pp. 147–72. Washington, D.C.: National Association for Education of Young Children.

Singer, J., ed. 1973. *The child's world of make-believe.* New York: Academic.

Smilansky, S. 1968. *The effects of socio-dramatic play on disadvantaged preschool children.* New York: Wiley.

Stevens, J. H., and King, E. W. 1976. *Administering early childhood education programs.* Boston: Little, Brown.

White, B. L. 1975. *The first three years of life.* New York: Avon.

Yawkey, T. D. 1981a. Project P.I.A.G.E.T. Promoting Intellectual Adaptation Given Experimental Transforming in Hispanic preschool children and their parents in center and home programs. Proposal submitted to the United States Department of Education, February 1981. Washington, D.C.

―――. 1981b. Sociodramatic play effects on mathematical learning and adult ratings of playfulness in five year olds. *Journal of Research and Development in Education.* 14:30–39.

Yawkey, T. D., and Prewitt-Diaz, J. O. 1981. Increasing minority parents' abilities in self help, play and language growth of their young handicapped children in home settings. In *Special education in action,* ed. W. Bell-Taylor, pp. 4–16. Washington, D.C.: International Business Machines, Inc.

Yawkey, T. D. and Silvern, S. B. 1977. Toward a comprehensive model for developmental curriculum and service evaluation as continued in early development and education of minority, handicapped and other special needs of children: some working hypotheses. The Wisconsin Department of Public Instruction, Madison, Wisconsin unclassified report for Dr. Sara Sherokow, 1–125.

Yawkey, T. D. and Yawkey, M. L. 1976. Racism, sexism, socioeconomic status, and story location of characters in selected picture books for young children. *Elementary English Journal* 53:545–48.

Parents and the Gifted Child

Sandra H. Heater

Coordinator of the gifted and talented program for the Ralston, Nebraska, public schools, Sandra H. Heater was formerly a Montessori directress, later a consultant in both early-childhood education and special education. Along with her work with the gifted and talented, she is also a reading specialist in the public schools of Nebraska. She is the author of Teaching Preschool Reading *(Brigham Young University Press, 1980).*

One hears occasionally of the prodigy who reads Shakespeare at the age of two. Such genius is extraordinary and also discomfiting. These children are so immediately recognizable that identification presents no problem. However, for the many lesser gifted youngsters, one must be more alert to their special talents. Early identification of the gifted and subsequent educational plans tailored to individual needs are essential components in the schooling of one of our most important resources.

For many years the prevalent attitude was that these very bright children would "get it on their own" without special programs. Indeed, it was not until 1972 that Congress created the Federal Office for the Talented and Gifted with the charge to educators to identify and help develop especially promising children. Progress has occurred in the search for these children and in creating appropriate educational services for them. Much, however, still remains to be done.

Perhaps 10 percent of the student population in the United States is gifted. Most school districts identify the top 3 to 5 percent, depending upon criteria. Whatever the numbers and selection procedures are, one cannot emphasize too strongly the need for early identification of gifted children. It is sheer profligacy to wait until the intermediate or higher grades to begin the specialized task of educating these children.

Whitmore (1980) lists four reasons for the establishment of early educational programs for gifted students. First, she believes that early identification and intervention are necessary to prevent under-achievement and social/emotional maladjustment. Second, early identi-fication maximizes the potential of each child. Third, early identi-fication permits expert help for those gifted children who have interfering handicaps that create great disparity between mental ability and physical capability. Fourth, early educational programing amelio-rates the effects of a disadvantaged environment, whether in the home or in a community of limited resources.

In order to provide early optimum educational stimulus for gifted children, schools and parents must be equally and effectively involved. The school is essential because, with its greater aggregate resources and trained personnel, it can provide more opportunities. Moreover, chil-dren spend significant amounts of time in school. If a gifted child infers that being gifted is acceptable, his self-concept is nurtured. Further-more, schools can continue and promote the interests brought from home. The school provides the chance for peer interaction and sharing, an important opportunity for gifted children who need the challenge of others.

The usual practice, partly from custom and partly from attitude, has been to exclude parents from school involvement at a meaningful level. Parents were welcome to form PTAs and serve as room mothers or oc-casional field trip chaperones but were not welcome when schools came to planning curriculum or identifying goals for the children's education.

To create and implement a gifted program, however, parents are an essential component. Often parents can provide the most imformation and offer the keenest insights into the children with whom the teachers work. Parental observations reveal interests to whet, strengths to aug-ment, and weaknesses to remediate, all of which, added to teacher knowledge, can make a significant difference in planning for the gifted child.

Parents as Partners

Parents of gifted children are sometimes anxious and tense. Part of the anxiety results from a heavy feeling of responsibility toward provid-ing every opportunity for their gifted child. Gifted children's barrage of questions and variety of interests are time consuming and involving. If there are less gifted children in the family, rivalries and unwholesome comparisons may result. Parents are often fearful of being considered "pushy" if they involve themselves in the school life of their child and guilt ridden if they do not become involved. For parents, life with a gifted child can be overwhelming.

There are support groups for parents of retarded or chronically ill children, but parents of gifted children usually receive little understanding of their special concerns. It is somehow presumptuous to ask for sympathy because of an unusually bright child. Parents realize that they must be especially careful in nurturing the child who very well may exhibit advanced—and disquieting—behavior.

Gifted children may dawdle irritatingly and lose track of time, a habit that aggravates parents. Sometimes these children use inappropriate means to get attention and may even bully other children. Gifted children frequently accept directions less readily without an explanation, a habit that grates on busy parents.

Parents often ask themselves questions such as, "Am I spending the right amount of time with my child?" "Am I doing the right sorts of things?" "Am I providing enriching experiences sufficient to meet the needs of my curious, ever eager-to-learn child?"

Sometimes an anxious parent will approach the teacher for advice or even for reassurance that everything is all right on the home front. If teachers and parents view themselves as dedicated partners allied to provide the very best learning climate, an honest, trust-inducing relationship can be built between family and school that will become one of the real sources of help available to gifted children. Close communication will bridge activities from school to home and vice versa, thus supplementing two major elements in the child's life.

Strongly organized, active parent groups are vital to the success of school programs for the gifted. Parents can move reluctant administrators or lagging school boards through means teachers are not free to use. Parents have been increasingly effective in garnering the support of state legislatures for gifted programs, and they can be a valuable resource in the classroom. For example, parents may be willing to demonstrate a hobby or discuss their profession with the students. They may act as mentors to other people's gifted children, or they may know of qthers who are willing to work individually with a gifted child outside the classroom. As volunteer aides and extra chaperones on field trips, parents can provide the support and practical help that encourages the teacher to do "extra" things. (However, to avoid a possible source of tension for all, parents should not aide regularly in their children's particular classroom.)

When parents and teachers view themselves and each other as cooperative team members allied for the purpose of creating maximum growth in gifted children, the link profits all concerned.

What, then, can the classroom teacher do to involve parents in ways that are mutually beneficial to home, school, and the child?

One very effective method is the individual education plan, or IEP. Many states have mandated IEPs for the handicapped student; now talented and gifted children are being served similarly. Soon, perhaps, IEPs will figure in all gifted education programs. However, until then, teachers should implement this program on their own.

Basically, an IEP involves a meeting including parent, teacher, and child, where the child discusses what he enjoys studying or wants to learn more about. The child is encouraged to be as candid as possible. Principals, counselors, and other concerned individuals can also be present. Together this team makes an assessment that will facilitate the development of a student's maximum potential. This united effort allies the two social units most influential in a pupil's life—the home and the school.

The teacher, other school officials, and parents discuss the student's strengths, weaknesses, interests, observed learning modalities, and personal and academic characteristics, as well as all other pertinent factors. Through this discussion, each can share observations made from a unique vantage point. Often teachers and parents surprise each other with observations of a child's behavior. By sharing the knowledge of what makes a child tick, all concerned have a clearer, more accurate perception of the youngster and thus can build a sounder educational plan for him or her. When parents share directly in planning and implementing their children's education, closer cooperation and support of the school ensues naturally.

Many forms of IEPs are possible. A teacher can either choose eclectically or design his own program for use within a class, school, or district. Whatever the format, the program should reflect the shared knowledge and common goals of student, parents, and teachers. When the child's program has been designed, everyone involved signs the document, thereby assuring each participant of mutual understanding and cooperation.

Another way parents and teachers can work together effectively is through specialized homework. The teacher sends home a brief explanation of what the child is learning in the classroom accompanied by suggested activities parents can help children do at home. A young gifted child may be very expressive, yet unable to write commensurately with his level of thought. Thus, the child can dictate stories, songs, or poems as the parent writes; and the parent can review punctuation, spelling, and structure with the child afterward. Such practice allows the young student to soar with fewer restraints. Parents also can support, encourage, and augment activities as their children work on independent study projects or after-school assignments. They can also explore other ways to facilitate the child's homework, keeping in mind segments of the homework the teacher wants the student to do without help.

Thus, regular communication between teacher and parents is necessary. An occasional telephone call or an informal note can supplement conferences to keep the exchange open.

Together teachers and parents can explore the benefits of bibliotherapy, a process whereby children explore their own emotions vicariously through the events in books. Frequently, gifted children feel different from other children, and they expend great effort to disguise their talents. When these children realize that others experience the same feelings, they can more easily accept their own uniqueness. Certainly parents can be valuable liaisons in this adjustment by reading and discussing with their children such works as *Encyclopedia Brown* (Sobol), *From the Mixed-up Files of Mrs. Basil E. Frankweiler* (Koningsburg), and *I Would Rather Be a Turnip* (Cleaver and Cleaver)—three of several possible selections that deal sensitively with the problems of the gifted.

Another area of parent-school alliance involves the creation of a pool of resources, human and material, that will expand learning opportunities. If parents do not want to act as mentors, for example, they may be able to suggest others who might do so; or they might provide other resource information. The entire school system benefits from this type of sharing.

To help parents help their gifted child, teachers can invite parents to attend workshops or seminars to increase their awareness of and support for gifted education. Parents will also appreciate book lists, materials catalogues, and creative suggestions for improving their own teaching and their support of their gifted child.

One of the most appropriate services a teacher can render parents is linking them with school counselors, who should also form part of the support team. Having a gifted child in the family can create as many disruptions in a family as having a handicapped child, and the need for effective counseling frequently exists. Teachers who have established a sound working relationship with parents can introduce counselors onto the working team.

Identification

In order to prepare and implement appropriate educational programs, teachers and parents must identify gifted students and their special talents, realizing that identification alone does not improve learning. Studies of both successful and unsuccessful gifted persons show that their achievement is based on a number of factors besides ability, including motivation, health, opportunities in the home and school, parent-child relationships, amount of interpersonal communication, nutrition, and other factors. However, these students and their abilities must be identified before their needs can be met. State and local educational agencies determine specific criteria for identification on which to establish their standards. A commonly used definition, although inter-preted in various ways throughout the fifty states, is the definition in *Education of the Gifted and Talented: Report to the Congress of the United States by the U.S. Commissioner of Education* (1971):

> *Gifted and talented children are those . . . who by virtue of out-standing abilities are capable of high performance. These are chil-dren who require differentiated educational programs and/or ser-vices beyond those normally provided by the regular school program in order to realize their contribution to self and society.*
>
> *Children capable of high performance include those with demon-strated achievement and/or potential ability in any of the follow-ing areas, singly or in combination:*
> 1. *general intellectual ability*
> 2. *specific academic ability*
> 3. *creative or productive thinking*
> 4. *leadership ability*
> 5. *visual and performing arts*
> 6. *psychomotor ability*°

Teachers and parents spend the greatest amount of time and exert the greatest influence on children during their early years. They must learn to perceive abilities, often despite inappropriate behavior or un-derachievement. A young child may, in achievement level, be four years beyond his grade without the adult's recognizing it because the child has learned to mask her abilities, has had no motivation, or is be-haviorally impaired. Identification is difficult because the young child is not likely to have created products that immediately evoke sparks of recognition from parents and teachers. Therefore, the adults in these children's lives must be especially attuned to elements of creativity that all too often masquerade as hyperactivity; incessant need to manipulate some aspect of the environment; fascination with colors, sound, or mu-sic; or, not infrequently, a "destructive" compulsion to disassemble ma-terials in an effort to explore. Sadly, the unidentified, unchanneled cre-ativity in a child is determined to be a discipline problem. His bright fires are ultimately squelched entirely.

Parents are often discounted as identifying sources because screening committees suspect them of bias. However, Jacobs (1971) and others have validated the ability of parents to nominate with accuracy their gifted children. Jacobs found that parent nomination of gifted kinder-garteners was 61 percent accurate. This contrasted with a teacher accu-racy rate of 9.5 percent. Thus, in the essential area of early identi-fication, parents must be heard.

°Some states, including Nebraska, are considering deleting this category from consideration in the education of the gifted children.

Tools of Identification

A variety of identification techniques exist. Standardized individual tests of intelligence, group achievement tests, tests to measure convergent thinking, the most common sort of thinking to measure, and tests to assess divergent or creative thinking are some of the measuring tools commonly used. Additionally there are evaluative measurements of feeling and tests of cultural differences.

The following tests are a partial list of instruments that teachers can use with young children. This is not an endorsement of any test, nor is it a complete list.

Convergent Thinking

Achievement
1. California Test of Basic Skills (1–8)
2. Iowa Test of Basic Skills (1–8)
3. Metropolitan Achievement Tests (1–9)
4. SRA Achievement Tests (1–12)
5. Stanford Achievement Tests (1–9)
6. Cognitive Abilities Test (K–8)

Intelligence
1. Stanford-Binet Intelligence Scale (K–12)
2. Wechsler Intelligence Scale for Children (WISC) (ages 5–15)
3. Peabody Picture Vocabulary Test (K–12)

Divergent Behavior
1. Torrance Test of Creative Thinking—Figural (1–12)
2. Personality Rating Scale
3. Preschool Academic Sentiment Scale (K–1)

Intelligence scores of 130 and above are used frequently to identify gifted children. Other school districts use a percentile cut-off of 96 or higher in a specific academic area on a standardized achievement test as an identifying criterion. These quantitative scores are comfortable to work with but too often overlook other areas of giftedness or penalize for ethnic differences or inequality of opportunity.

There is no one "correct" instrument that has universal validity and reliability. Very often, in fact, means of identification other than tests are especially effective in recognizing very young talented and gifted children. One popular instrument is the Renzulli-Hartman Scale for Rating Behavioral Characteristics of Superior Students.° Parent evaluations, peer nomination, self-nomination, and sociograms are further ways of identifying the talented and gifted youngsters. Each instrument has strengths and weaknesses.

°Available in a document from the National/State Leadership Training Institute, 316 West Second Street, PH-C, Los Angeles, CA 90012.

For example, individual intelligence tests are very good since quality of performance can be interpreted, a broader sampling of abilities tested, and the testing environment controlled. Their disadvantages are time, cost, and possible cultural bias.

Group intelligence tests are a faster, cheaper way to test large numbers to indicate the need for further testing. However, poor readers are penalized on group tests, and the underachievers and culturally deprived may score too low to be noticed.

Peer and self-nominations occasionally are quite accurate if the child is old enough for self-awareness and for the observation of others; however, children often conceal their abilities. Gifted children, as we have said, may consider themselves to be "different" and will try hard not to be.

The most accurate identification procedure includes the use of several of the above evaluative tools. And until the flawless instrument is designed, the teacher of young children must be especially perceptive and discerning to see the potential of these special learners and must draw upon the observation of parents to help in the identification and education process.

To help parents and teachers know what characteristics to look for to identify gifted children, Roger Taylor (1976) and others have compiled inventories and screening questionnaires for use by parents, teachers, and students themselves.

The following is a general screening questionnaire for teachers:

General Screening Questionnaire for the Gifted and Talented

Teacher   Level   Date

Compare the students in your class. List below the three students who display the greatest amount of talent or ability in each area.

Intelligence	1 _____ 2 _____ 3 _____
Creativity	1 _____ 2 _____ 3 _____
Positive self-concept	1 _____ 2 _____ 3 _____
Athletic ability	1 _____ 2 _____ 3 _____
Artistic ability	1 _____ 2 _____ 3 _____
Verbal ability	1 _____ 2 _____ 3 _____
Problem-solving ability	1 _____ 2 _____ 3 _____
Leadership ability	1 _____ 2 _____ 3 _____
Reading ability	1 _____ 2 _____ 3 _____
Math ability	1 _____ 2 _____ 3 _____
Knowledge	1 _____ 2 _____ 3 _____
Motivation to learn	1 _____ 2 _____ 3 _____
Personality	1 _____ 2 _____ 3 _____

Popularity	1 _____	2 _____	3 _____
Initiative	1 _____	2 _____	3 _____
Awareness of others	1 _____	2 _____	3 _____
Science aptitude	1 _____	2 _____	3 _____

Other practical checklists available to kindergarten and first-grade teachers are these two items adapted from James Miley, coordinator for the gifted in the Dade County, Florida, Public Schools.

Checklist for Kindergarten

Directions: Please place an X in the space beside each question which *best* describes the pupil.

	YES	NO
A. Language		
1. The pupil is able to read.	_____	_____
2. The pupil understands his relationship in such words as up-down, top-bottom, big-little, far-near.	_____	_____
B. Psychomotor Abilities		
1. The pupil exhibits coordination by being able to bounce a ball or tie his shoelaces.	_____	_____
2. The pupil can complete the missing parts of an incomplete familiar picture by drawing the parts in their proper perspective.	_____	_____
C. Mathematics		
1. The pupil can repeat five digits forward and backward.	_____	_____
2. The pupil recognizes and understands the value of coins (penny, nickle, dime and quarter).	_____	_____
D. Creativity		
1. The pupil interprets stories or pictures in his own words.	_____	_____
2. The pupil displays curiosity by asking many questions or by other types of behavior.	_____	_____
E. General Characteristics		
1. The pupil readily adapts to new situations; he is flexible in thought and action; he seems undisturbed when the normal routine is changed.	_____	_____
2. The pupil seeks new tasks and activities.	_____	_____
3. The pupil tends to dominate others and generally directs the activity in which he is involved.	_____	_____

Checklist for First Grade Pupils

Directions: Please place an X in the space beside each question which
best describes the pupil.

	YES	NO
1. The pupil reads two years above grade level.		
2. The pupil recognizes the number and sequences of steps in a specified direction.		
3. The pupil forms sets and subsets.		
4. The pupil understands the concepts of place value.		
5. The pupil recognizes the properties of right angles.		
6. The pupil can create a short story from a familiar subject.		
7. The pupil interprets stories and pictures in his own words.		
8. The pupil questions critically.		
9. The pupil demonstrates flexibility in his thinking pattern and the ability to communicate with others.		
10. The pupil is self-confident with pupils his own age and adults; seems comfortable when asked to show his work to class.		
11. The pupil has a well-developed vocabulary.		
12. The pupil has a vivid imagination and enjoys sharing his stories with others.		

E. P. Torrance (1962) has designed a questionnaire to which each
classroom teacher can respond with the directions to nominate the
following:
Best student
Child with the biggest vocabulary
Most creative and original
Child with the most leadership
Most scientifically oriented child
Child who does the best critical thinking
Able child who is the biggest nuisance
Best motivated child
Child the other children like best
Child who is most ahead on grade placement
Brightest child of a minority group of more than five members who has
     not been named in any of the above categories
Child whose parents are most concerned about the enrichment of his
     educational process.

Even without checklists and tests, the alert teacher can note certain characteristics that most gifted children display either constantly or intermittently. These sorts of behaviors are enumerated in some form by nearly every authority in the field. Among the traits to watch for are these:

Unusual maturity in observation
Highly developed powers of concentration
High degree of independent thinking
Versatile use of mental processes
Perseverance in intellectual endeavors
Desire to learn
Mastery of basic skills
Excellent or precocious use of language
Creative imagination and resourcefulness
Alertness and responsiveness with heightened sensitivity to the immediate environment
Ability to organize information
Widely varied interest
Intense curiosity in one or more areas
Ability to grasp abstract generalizations
Insight into problems
Retention of information
Extreme rapidity in learning and remembering
Ability to tell a story
Tendency to reproduce accurately the correct sequence of happenings during a field trip or event
Cooperative behavior
High quality of participation in school activities
Leadership

No one child will exhibit all of these traits even part of the time. An occasional youngster's giftedness lies heavily in one area, and the child usually concentrates on activities in that field. Other children have a broader-based range of interests, experiencing difficulty in limiting themselves to few enough interests.

Often children can help identify gifted classmates. Even very young children can respond to questions such as these:

Which boys or girls in your class do you usually choose to play games with?
Which girls or boys in your class often suggest new games to play or things to do?
Which children in your class usually have ideas about things in your class?
Who usually explains new things to others in your group?
Who usually does things differently?

Frequently the responses children give are sound indicators of which students to examine closely as potentially gifted. Parents, too, can provide invaluable insight necessary for identifying gifted children. The following checklist can be sent home to parents and will provide useful information in planning. This checklist also focuses parents' attention on their children's behavior and forces some close scrutiny.

Parent Inventory

A. What special talents or skills does your child have?

Give examples of behavior that illustrate this.

B. Check the following items that best describe your child as you see him or her.

	Little	Some	Great Deal
1. Is alert beyond his years			
2. Likes school			
3. Has interests of older children or of adults in games and reading			
4. Sticks to a project once it is started			
5. Is observant			
6. Has lots of ideas to share			
7. Has many different ways of solving problems			
8. Is aware of problems others often do not see			
9. Uses unique and unusual ways of solving problems			
10. Wants to know how and why			
11. Likes to pretend			
12. Other children call him/her to initiate play activities			
13. Asks a lot of questions about a variety of subjects			
14. Is not concerned with details			
15. Enjoys and responds to beauty			
16. Is able to plan and organize activities			
17. Has above-average coordination, agility and ability in organized games			
18. Often finds and corrects own mistakes			
19. Others seem to enjoy his/her company			
20. Makes up stories and has ideas that are unique			

21. Has a wide range of interests   _____ _____ _____
22. Gets other children to do what he/she wants   _____ _____ _____
23. Likes to play organized games and is good at them   _____ _____ _____
24. Enjoys other people and seeks them out   _____ _____ _____
25. Is able and willing to work with others   _____ _____ _____
26. Sets high standards for self   _____ _____ _____
27. Chooses difficult problems over simple ones   _____ _____ _____
28. Is able to laugh at himself (if necessary)   _____ _____ _____
29. Likes to do many things and participates whole-heartedly   _____ _____ _____
30. Likes to have his/her ideas known   _____ _____ _____

C. Reading interests (favorite type of books and/or titles of favorite books) _____

D. Favorite school subject _____

E. General attitude toward school _____

F. Favorite playtime, leisure time activity _____

G. Hobbies and special interests (collections, dancing, making models, swimming, singing, painting, cooking, sewing, drama, etc.) _____
_____

H. What special lessons, training, or learning opportunities does your child have outside of school? _____
_____

I. What are some of the influences at home or at school that may negatively influence your child's performance in school? _____
_____

J. What other things would you like us to know that would assist us in planning a program for your child? _____
_____

When such processes of identification are used in addition to the more formal approaches, the likelihood exists that a gifted child will be recognized despite possible problems, such as being a slow reader, a classroom nuisance, or culturally deprived.

Conditions for Creative Teaching

Teachers must teach parents how to teach and work with their children.

Smith (1966) believed that creativity cannot be taught but, instead, that creativity is inherent and can only be developed. While certain facets of creative processes can be modified as all learning can be modified, creativity as a separate entity must be nurtured and developed very carefully. Certain conditions seem to evoke creative elements in children. If this is true, parents and teachers must provide the stimuli that causes creativity to appear and reappear.

Hilgard (1959) discussed four categories that tend to develop creativity: (1) intellectual conditions; (2) physical conditions; (3) social and emotional conditions; and (4) psychological conditions.

Certainly the home can stimulate development in each of these areas by the actions and examples of the parents. A family need not be wealthy to explore such intellectually stimulating areas as libraries, zoos, nature, or the neighborhood. Talking with children and answering questions patiently are good ways to encourage intellectual growth. Children need space to run in or to build a private place. Daily outdoor exercise with unrestricted movement allows children to develop physically and mentally at the same time. When a child can feel good about himself and receives positive reenforcement from parents or other family members, he grows psychologically and emotionally. Youngsters require exposure to a variety of social situations to become confident of their ability to function outside the family. Parents should include children in as many social settings as possible.

Daily life provides many opportunities for parents to develop creativity in their children. Such development often occurs naturally. However, parents may also contrive situations to foster creativity. For example, a camping experience can be used to encourage exploration, self-reliance, interaction with family members, and physical activity. Parents can start the outing with the purpose of developing their children's curiosity and coping skills.

Teachers, too, use the natural environment of the classroom to foster creativity. Opportunities for spontaneous reaction happen frequently where young children are. Just as parents can use a contrived experience, teachers can also contrive lesson plans to teach students to think and produce creatively.

This is not to disparage the necessity of convergent thinking processes. Indeed, even the most able student has to have a basis to spring from, but to exclude divergent creative thought from learning is to stifle some of the finest potential.

Research has shown that one of the most effective of all teaching strategies and one of the best ways to help students develop both types of thinking, convergent and divergent, is the use of questions that require thinking. These questions require the students to apply, analyze, synthesize, and evaluate knowledge, rather than merely parrot back information. Most recent education graduates have a working knowledge of Bloom's Taxonomy (1956), a descriptive hierarchy of cognitive processes and a base for good questioning sequences. Below is a brief description of the major categories in the cognitive domain as discussed by Bloom.

1. *Knowledge* is the remembering of previously learned material. This is the lowest level of learning outcomes in the cognitive domain.
2. *Comprehension* is the ability to grasp the meaning of material. This goes one step beyond the simple remembering of material.
3. *Application* is the ability to use learned material in new and concrete situations. This level is higher in the hierarchy of understanding than the level of comprehension.
4. *Analysis* is the ability to break down material into its component parts in order to understand the organizational structure. Learning outcomes here are at a higher intellectual level than comprehension and application because they require an understanding of content and the structure of the material.
5. *Synthesis* is the ability to restructure parts to form a new whole. Learning outcomes in this area stress creative behaviors with the major emphasis on formulating new patterns or structures.
6. *Evaluation* is the ability to judge the value of material for a given purpose with judgments based on definite criteria. Learning outcomes are highest in this area because they contain elements of all the other categories, in addition to conscious value judgments based on clearly defined criteria.

Young children are capable of these cognitive processes and benefit from questions that recognize more advanced levels of thought.

Open-ended questioning can stimulate divergent thinking in addition to the application of Bloom's Taxonomy. Teachers or parents might use such questioning models as these:

1. How many ways . . . ? List all of the _____ .
2. How is a _____ like a _____ ?
3. How would you feel if you were a _____ ?
4. What if you had eyes in the back of your head?
5. If you could do anything right now, what would you do?
6. What if there were no birds?

Infinite variations of these sorts of questions pique young minds into creative thinking, often evoking exciting spin-off ideas and interests. Parents are in an excellent position to ask these kinds of questions, leading children into higher-level thinking.

Unfortunately, 85 percent of classroom questions fall into either the knowledge or comprehension categories, thereby depriving children of an opportunity to think divergently and creatively.

Another method to help children learn to think creatively is Future Problem Solving. E. Paul Torrance (1962) has devised some problem-solving techniques and activities that a number of elementary schools presently use.°

°Further information is available from all state departments of education as well as the University of Georgia, Athens, Georgia.

Very briefly, students learn to examine the elements of a problem, to identify the problem, and then to arrive at a solution. For example, youngsters receive many facts on a topic but no specific problem. Instead, the students have to pick out the problem hidden among the facts. After identifying the problem, the youngsters explore every possible solution, probable or improbable, then sift through solutions to find the best one. This sort of activity encourages children to think creatively and to explore many options before making a decision. Parents can use these same techniques.

Parents of the Talented and Gifted

What are beneficial characteristics that parents of gifted children should have? Certain traits appear to be helpful:

Intelligence. Parents do not have to be gifted themselves, but a keen intelligence is helpful.

Flexibility in approach to life. Gifted children present constant challenges that require parental flexibility.

Positive attitude. Parents should believe that a gifted child is a blessing and not a curse.

Strong self-concept. Parents should feel secure about themselves and about their own decision-making abilities.

Wide variety of interests. Interests of parents can stimulate children to pursue their own interests and to explore widely.

Well-developed curiosity. It is good to let children see that parents, too, are avid learners and askers of questions.

Patience. Gifted children, especially, can try parents' patience, and parents often need extra amounts to cope with their children's exploring, questing natures.

Sense of humor. One characteristic of gifted children can be a sharp sense of humor. It is helpful if parents also have a well-developed sense of humor, both as an example and for self preservation.

Fairness. This includes looking objectively at all children in the family and not comparing one with another. Fairness also involves recognizing that gifted youngsters, bright though they are, are still children who will act childishly, babyishly even, at times. Gifted children do not always bring home perfect report cards and first prizes.

Actually, the techniques of sound parenting apply to the child of any ability level. Too often, however, the parents of the gifted child get so caught up in the responsibilities of rearing him that they lose part of the pleasure.

Parents of gifted children should encourage the interests of their children, even when those interests are not appealing to the parents. Of course, the parent must determine the safety of such things as scientific experiments and must supervise closely as necessary.

For the gifted child who is a perfectionist and is self-demanding, the parent should provide support and assurance that perfection is not always necessary. For the underachieving gifted child the parent has to be an occasional prod. Balance is necessary with a gifted child, and parents are the logical ones to provide that.

Parents should inform themselves about gifted children. Here the school personnel can be valuable resources, but parents can also help each other in support groups, and they can use books and workshops to learn how gifted children think and react.

For home and school alike, a partnership between the two is an invaluable tool. When parent and teacher understand the role each plays in educating the gifted, better programs develop.

Administrative Arrangements and Program Alternatives

Schools use several approaches to educate gifted children. The arrangement depends on school design, staff, enrollment, finances, and administration. No one best way exists for all schools, and parents should be informed of program alternatives. Often the administration makes the decision, but parents need to understand why a certain option was chosen and why this appears best for a particular school. Here are some common alternatives for educating gifted children.

Grouping places students of like ability together. Some schools provide time for gifted students to work only with each other.

Acceleration means that students work through a subject area or grade faster than normal. A second grade child might go into third grade math at midyear, for example.

Enrichment provides broader, deeper study of a topic. Enrichment works well with individual students who show strong interests in an area that can be anything from dinosaurs to computers.

Early entrance allows a child to enter kindergarten before the legal entrance age. Parents and teachers both need to be involved in this decision, which is far reaching. The child will always be young for her grade, a fact that may be important socially. Usually a parent requests testing for early entrance because the child is reading independently or appears very advanced over her age mates.

Multiple age grouping mixes children of various ages, such as five through seven or seven through nine. The purpose of this arrangement is to let gifted young children associate with older students who are doing more advanced work.

Homogeneous classes put together children of comparable ability. In these classes all gifted students are placed together. Advantages are peer stimulus and fast pacing, but a disadvantage is loss of association with a variety of other students.

Often, a school uses combinations of these techniques that may change from year to year. Informed parents are essential for the support of any of these arrangements. Parents' questions should be encouraged to promote understanding of what occurs at school.

Some At-Home Activities

Kits, games, puzzles, and activities serve a useful purpose in education of the gifted. Parents recognize early that their children's wonderfully fertile minds respond to a variety of techniques, often with surprising insight and freshness.

Books provide the family with a way to encourage gifted children. Family reading time allows each person to share part of a book or story. The beginning reader observes that the entire family is excited about books and reading; in turn, his own interest in books is whetted.

Increasing numbers of computer games are available. In this computer age all children need early exposure to such tools. Parents can provide their child opportunities to use computers by taking him to displays and to their offices, or by buying inexpensive computer games that children seem to love.

Some computer aids to consider are Texas Instruments' "Little Professor," a gadget that resembles a hand-held calculator with big keys and a bright plastic face. Little Professor gives problems and then corrects answers, functioning as an electronic flash card for mathematics practice and drill. Other Texas Instrument products are "Speak & Spell," "Speak & Math," and "Speak & Read." Imitating human speech, these three machines ask questions and then calmly prod, correct, or reward, depending on the answers received.

Coleco has produced the "Electronic Learning Machine." Correct responses elicit green lights and happy times, while incorrect answers receive red lights and unhappy times. Mattel's "Children's Discovery System" includes a keyboard, musical sound effects, and animation on a viewing screen that tries to teach not only spelling and vocabulary but also music and art. These descriptions are merely a sampling of what is on the market and are not endorsements of any product. (Education Products Information Exchange (EPIE) has prepared a report on computer learning aids for Ford Foundation.)

If a child's interest is science, many science kits and tools are available for experiment. One of the best is a simple ten-power hand lens microscope that can open the door to a world of exploration. Gifted youngsters also enjoy comparing American and metric measurement. Simple measuring cups, a meter stick, and a yard stick are enough to stimulate comparisons and conclusion drawing.

A life-long interest in science can begin very young. Parents can use a book to supply the botanical names of common plants. This leads to discovery searches, classifying, and collecting.

The budding author who cannot yet write can dictate poems or stories that parents turn into books with the help of the child, who may illustrate her work also.

Teachers can share information about companies or products that make materials for gifted children. While materials are helpful, there is no substitute for parental time, interest, conversation, and question asking and answering. Time for children to explore, to daydream, and to feel is essential.

Conclusion

One major factor affecting increased awareness and support of the gifted child has been parental involvement. Authorities are pointing to research that demonstrates the ability of parents to identify their gifted children, and the trend is increasingly toward parents as major partners in designing curriculum for their highly capable offspring.

Mutually agreed-upon goals and a cooperative spirit between the potent forces of home and school will do much to create a nurturing environment for an invaluable resource—the gifted child.

References

Abraham, Willard. 1976. Counseling the gifted. *Focus/Guidance* 1:9.

Bloom, Benjamin S. 1956. Taxonomy of educational objectives: the classification of educational goals. *Handbook I: Cognitive Domain,* ed. B. S. Bloom, pp. 254–57. New York: David McKay Co.

Gallagher, J. J. 1975. *Teaching the gifted child.* Boston: Allyn and Bacon.

Guilford, J. P. 1950. Creativity. *American Psychologist* 5:444–54.

Hilgard, E. 1959. Creativity and problem solving. In *Interdisciplinary Symposia on Creativity,* ed. Harold H. Anderson, pp. 179–80. New York: Harper and Row.

Jacobs, J. C. 1971. Effectiveness of teacher and parent identification of gifted children as a function of school levels. *Psychology in the Schools* 8:140–42.

Renzulli, J. S. and Smith, L. H. 1977. Two approaches to identification of gifted students. *Exceptional Children* 3:512–18.

Smith, James A. 1966. *Setting conditions for creative teaching in the elementary school.* Boston: Allyn & Bacon.

Taylor, Roger. 1976. *The gifted and talented.* Englewood, Colorado: Educational Consulting Associates.

Torrance, E. P. 1962. Non-test ways of identifying the creatively gifted. *The Gifted Child Quarterly* 6:71–75.

Whitmore, Ann. 1980. *Giftedness, conflict, and underachievement.* Boston: Allyn and Bacon.